COMPLETE

Baking

p

Note
Cup measurements in this book are for American cups.
Tablespoons are assumed to be 15 ml. Unless otherwise stated,
milk is assumed to be whole, eggs are large,
and pepper is freshly ground black pepper.

Contents

Introduction

This beautifully illustrated book brings you all the skills you need to recreate some of the best-loved traditional baking dishes. It also shows you how to experiment with some of the exciting contemporary ingredients now readily available in leading supermarkets.

Clear step-by-step instructions guide you through the techniques needed to mastermind all those baking favorites that have been savored and enjoyed from generation to generation.

FAMILY FAVORITES

Experience the sweet pleasure of a wonderful selection of everyday and special occasion desserts and rich, gooey and irresistible puddings in Chapter 3, such Pavlova, Black Forest Trifle, Queen of Puddings and Crème Brûlée Tarts. Your favorite is sure to be included.

This chapter also helps you to perfect your pastry so that you are guaranteed success with such timeless appetizing cookery classics as Treacle Tart, Apple Tart Tatin, Apricot and Cranberry Frangipane and Egg Custard Tart.

BREADS & SAVORIES

Making bread at home is great fun and allows you to experiment with all sorts of ingredients, such as sun-dried tomatoes, garlic, mangoes and olive oil, to create versatile and delicious variations of modern breads, rolls and loaves. Chapter 4 also shows you how to spice-up all sorts of savories with exciting adaptations of traditional flans, pies and biscuits, such as Curry Pasties, tasty Asparagus & Goats Cheese Tart, Red Onion Tart Tatin and delicious Celery & Onion pies.

VEGETARIAN COOKING

Vegetarian recipes full of delicious wholesome ingredients, which are every bit as good as traditional baking favorites, have been created in Chapter 4. Recipes include Lentil & Red Bell Pepper Flan, Date & Apricot Tart, Pineapple Upside-down Cake and Brazil Nut & Mushroom Pie.

CAKES & COOKIES

Transform traditional cakes and cookies into a real tea-time extravaganza with some new adaptations of old tea-time favorites in Chapters 1 and 2.

Irresistible cake recipes, such as Marbled Chocolate Cake, Olive Oil Fruit & Nut Cake, Gingerbread and Apple Shortcakes, are included as are delicious cookie recipes, such as Chocolate Chip Cookies and Ginger Cookies. These are quick and easy to make and are sure to be winners with all the family.

MAKING CAKES

With all baking recipes, there are some basic principles that apply and this is especially true of cake making:

- First of all make sure that you read the recipe all the way through.

- Weigh all ingredients accurately and do basic preparation, such as grating and chopping, before starting cooking.

- Basic cake-making ingredients should kept be at room temperature.

- Mixtures that are creamed together, such as butter and sugar, should be almost white and have a 'soft dropping' consistency. Creaming can be done by hand, but a hand-held electric mixer saves time and effort.

- 'Folding in' is achieved by using a metal spoon or spatula and working as gently as possible to fold through the flour or dry ingredients in a figure of eight movement.

- Do not remove a cake from the oven until it is fully cooked. To test if a cake is cooked, press the surface lightly with your fingertips – it should feel springy to the touch. Alternatively, insert a fine metal skewer into the center of the cake – it will come out clean if the cake is cooked through.

- Leave cakes in their pans to cool before carefully turning out on to a wire rack to cool completely.

MAKING PIES & TARTS

When making the pies or tarts in the book, follow these basic principles:

- Sift the dry ingredients into a large mixing bowl, add the diced fat and toss it through the flour.

- Gently rub the fat between your fingertips a little at a time until the mixture looks like fine bread crumbs and, as you rub in the mixture, lift your hands up to aerate the mixture as it falls back into the bowl.

- Bind the mixture with iced water or other liquid, using just enough to make a soft dough. Wrap the dough and leave to chill for at least 30 minutes.

Cooking with Chocolate

Chocolate is one of life's luxuries and one of the few that we can all afford. This book contains all of the recipes you need to enjoy this luxury at any time of the day. For example, you could wake up to Pain au Chocolat, or have a tasty chocolate cookie with morning coffee. You could indulge in a hot chocolate pudding at lunch time, have a sumptuous slice of chocolate cake with afternoon tea, luxuriate with a rich chocolate dessert as part of the evening meal and round off the end of the day with a hot chocolate toddy. Whilst this might seem to be taking things too far, even for the most hardened chocoholic, why not tempt yourself with a perfect chocolate treat now and then. Go on spoil yourself!

Chocolate is produced from the beans of the cacao tree, which originated in South America, but now grows in Africa, the West Indies, the tropical parts of America and the Far East. Cacao beans are large pods – once harvested, both the pulp from the pods and the bean are allowed to ferment in the sun. The pulp evaporates and the bean develops it's chocolatey flavor. The outer skin is then removed and the beans are left in the sun for a little longer or roasted. Finally, they are shelled and the nibs are used for making cocoa and chocolate.

The nibs have to be ground and processed to produce a thick mixture or paste called "cocoa solids" and it is this that we refer to when gauging the quality of chocolate. The cocoa solids are then pressed to remove some of the fat – 'cocoa butter'. They are then further processed to produce the product that we know and love as chocolate.

STORING CHOCOLATE

Store chocolate in a cool, dry place away from direct heat or sunlight. Most chocolate can be stored for about 1 year. It can be stored in the refrigerator, but make sure it is well wrapped as it will pick up flavors from other foods. Chocolate decorations can be stored in airtight containers and interleaved with non-stick baking parchment. Dark chocolate will keep for 4 weeks and milk and white chocolate for 2 weeks.

MELTING CHOCOLATE

Chocolate should not be melted over direct heat, except when melted with other ingredients and even then the heat should be very low.

Break the chocolate into small, equal-sized pieces and place them in a heatproof bowl. Place over a pan of hot water, making sure the base is not in contact with the water. Once the chocolate starts to melt, stir gently and if necessary leave over the water a little longer. No drops of water or steam should come into contact with the melted chocolate as it will solidify.

To melt chocolate in the microwave, break the chocolate into small pieces and place in a microwave-proof bowl. Timing will vary according to the type and quantity of chocolate. As a guide, melt 4$\frac{1}{2}$ oz dark chocolate on High for 2 minutes and white or milk chocolate for 2-3 minutes on Medium. Stir the chocolate and leave to stand for a few minutes, then stir again. Return to the microwave for a further 30 seconds if necessary.

SETTING CHOCOLATE

Chocolate sets best at 65°F although it will set (more slowly) in a slightly hotter room. If possible set chocolate for decorations in a cool room. If set in the refrigerator it may develop a white bloom.

TYPES OF CHOCOLATE

Dark Chocolate *can contain anything from 30% to 75% cocoa solids. It has a slightly sweet flavor and a dark color. It is the chocolate most used in cooking. For everyday cooking and the majority of these recipes calling for dark chocolate, choose one with around 50% cocoa solids. However, dark chocolate with a higher cocoa solid content will give a richer more intense flavor. This chocolate is often called luxury or continental chocolate and has a cocoa solid content of between 70-75%. Occasionally it is essential to use a better chocolate and I have indicated in the individual recipes where this is the case.*

Milk Chocolate, *as its name suggests, contains milk and has a lovely creamy, mild and sweet flavor. It is mostly used as an eating chocolate, rather than in cooking. However it does have it's place in chocolate cookery, especially for decorations and when a milder, creamy flavor is required. It is more sensitive to heat than dark chocolate so care must be taken when melting it.*

White Chocolate *contains a lower cocoa butter content and cocoa solids. It can be quite temperamental when used in cooking.*

Always choose a luxury cooking white chocolate to avoid problems and take great care not to overheat when melting. White chocolate is useful for color contrast especially when decorating cakes.

Couverture, *although this is the preferred chocolate for professionals (it retains a high gloss after melting and cooling) it requires tempering and is only available from specialist suppliers and has therefore not been used in this book.*

Chocolate-flavored Cake Covering *is an inferior product not generally used by true chocolate lovers. However it has a higher fat content making it easier to handle when making some decorations, such as curls or caraque. If you do not want to compromise the flavor too much, but have difficulty making the decorations with pure chocolate, try adding a few squares of chocolate-flavored cake covering to a good quality chocolate.*

Chocolate Chips *are available in dark, milk and white chocolate varieties and are used for baking and decoration.*

Cocoa Powder *is the powder left after the cocoa butter has been pressed from the roasted and ground beans. It is unsweetened and bitter in flavor. It gives a good, strong chocolate flavor.*

Cakes & Gateaux

It is hard to resist the pleasure of a sumptuous piece of chocolate cake and no chocolate book would be complete without a selection of family cakes and gateaux – there are plenty to choose from in this chapter. You can spend several indulgent hours in the kitchen making that perfect extravagant gateau or pop into the kitchen to knock up a quick cake for afternoon tea, the choice is yours. The more experimental among you can vary the fillings or decorations used according to what takes your fancy.

Alternatively, follow our easy step-by-step directions and look at our glossy pictures to guide you to perfect results. The gateaux in this book will be just at home on the dessert table – they are a feast for the eyes and will keep all hardened chocoholics in ecstasy. The family cakes are ideal for those who find a slice of chocolate cake comforting at any time, as many of them are made with surprising ease. So next time you feel like an indulgent slice of melt-in-the-mouth chocolate cake look no further.

Gingerbread

*This spicy gingerbread is made even more moist
by the addition of chopped fresh apples.*

Makes 12 bars

INGREDIENTS

$^2/_3$ cup butter
1 cup soft brown sugar
2 tbsp black molasses
2 cups all-purpose flour

1 tsp baking powder
2 tsp baking soda
2 tsp ground ginger
$^2/_3$ cup milk

1 egg, beaten
2 dessert apples, peeled, chopped and
　　coated with 1 tbsp lemon juice

1 Grease a 9 inch square cake pan and line with baking parchment.

2 Melt the butter, sugar, and molasses in a saucepan over a low heat and leave the mixture to cool.

3 Sift the flour, baking powder, baking soda, and ginger into a mixing bowl.

4 Stir in the milk, beaten egg and cooled buttery liquid, followed by the chopped apples coated with the lemon juice.

5 Mix everything together gently, then pour the mixture into the prepared pan.

6 Bake in a preheated oven, 325°F, for 30-35 minutes until the cake has risen and a fine skewer inserted into the center comes out clean.

7 Leave the cake to cool in the pan before turning out and cutting into 12 bars.

VARIATION

*If you enjoy the flavor of ginger, try
adding 1 oz candied ginger,
chopped finely,
to the mixture in step 3.*

Almond Cake

Being glazed with a honey syrup after baking gives this almond-flavored cake a lovely moist texture, but it can be eaten without the glaze, if preferred.

Serves 8

INGREDIENTS

$^1/_3$ cup soft tub margarine
3 tbsp soft brown sugar
2 eggs
$1^1/_2$ cups self-rising flour
1 tsp baking powder

4 tbsp milk
2 tbsp runny honey
$^1/_2$ cup flaked almonds

SYRUP:
$^2/_3$ cup runny honey
2 tbsp lemon juice

1 Grease an 7 inch round cake pan and line with baking parchment.

2 Place the margarine, brown sugar, eggs, flour, baking powder, milk, and honey in a large mixing bowl and beat well with a wooden spoon for about 1 minute until all of the ingredients are thoroughly mixed together.

3 Spoon into the prepared pan, level the surface with the back of a spoon or a knife, and sprinkle with the almonds.

4 Bake in a preheated oven, 350°F, for about 50 minutes or until the cake is well risen.

5 Meanwhile, make the syrup. Combine the honey and lemon juice in a small saucepan and simmer for about 5 minutes or until the syrup starts to coat the back of a spoon.

6 As soon as the cake comes out of the oven, pour over the syrup, allowing it to seep into the middle of the cake.

7 Leave the cake to cool for at least 2 hours before slicing.

COOK'S TIP

Experiment with different flavored honeys for the syrup glaze until you find one that you think tastes best.

Coffee & Almond Streusel Cake

*This cake has a moist coffee sponge on the bottom,
covered with a crisp crunchy, spicy topping.*

Serves 8

INGREDIENTS

1¼ cups all-purpose flour
1 tbsp baking powder
⅓ cup superfine sugar
⅔ cup milk
2 eggs
½ cup butter, melted and cooled
2 tbsp instant coffee mixed with
   1 tbsp boiling water
⅓ cup almonds, chopped

confectioners' sugar, for dusting

TOPPING:
½ cup self-rising flour
⅓ cup brown crystal sugar
6 tsp butter, cut into
   small pieces

1 tsp ground allspice
1 tbsp water

1 Grease a 9 inch loose-bottomed round cake pan and line with baking parchment. sift together the flour and baking powder into a mixing bowl, then stir in the superfine sugar.

2 Whisk the milk, eggs, butter, and coffee mixture together and pour on to the dry ingredients. Add the chopped almonds and mix lightly together. Spoon the mixture into the pan.

3 To make the topping, mix the flour and brown crystal sugar together in a separate bowl.

4 Rub in the butter with your fingers until the mixture is crumbly. Sprinkle in the ground allspice and the water and bring the mixture together in loose crumbs. Sprinkle the topping over the cake mixture.

5 Bake in a preheated oven, 375°F, for 50 minutes-1 hour. Cover loosely with foil if the topping starts to brown too quickly. Leave to cool in the pan, then turn out. Dust with confectioners' sugar just before serving.

Marbled Chocolate Cake

Separate chocolate and orange cake mixtures are combined in the ring mold to achieve the marbled effect in this light sponge.

Serves 8

INGREDIENTS

3/4 cup butter, softened
3/4 cup superfine sugar
3 eggs, beaten

1¼ cups self-rising flour, sifted
¼ cup cocoa powder, sifted

5-6 tbsp orange juice
grated rind of 1 orange

1 Lightly grease a 10 inch ovenproof ring mold.

2 In a mixing bowl, cream together the butter and sugar with an electric whisk for about 5 minutes.

3 Add the beaten egg a little at a time, whisking well after each addition.

4 Using a metal spoon, fold the flour into the creamed mixture carefully, then spoon half of the mixture into a separate mixing bowl.

5 Fold the cocoa powder and half of the orange juice into one bowl and mix gently.

6 Fold the orange rind and remaining orange juice into the other bowl and mix gently.

7 Place spoonfuls of each of the mixtures alternately into the mold, then drag a skewer through the mixture to create a marbled effect.

8 Bake in a preheated oven, 350°F, for 30-35 minutes until well risen and a skewer inserted into the center comes out clean.

9 Leave the cake to cool in the mold before turning out on to a wire rack.

VARIATION

For a richer chocolate flavor, add 1¾ oz chocolate drops to the cocoa mixture.

5

6

7

Apple Shortcakes

This traditional American dessert is a freshly baked sweet scone, split and filled with sliced apples and whipped cream. The shortcakes can be eaten warm or cold.

Serves 8

INGREDIENTS

1¼ cups all-purpose flour
½ tsp salt
1 tsp baking powder
1 tbsp superfine sugar
1 tbsp butter, cut into
    small pieces

¼ cup milk
confections' sugar, for dusting

FILLING:
3 eating apples, peeled, cored,
    and sliced

½ cup superfine sugar
1 tbsp lemon juice
1 tsp ground cinnamon
1⅓ cups water
⅔ cup heavy cream, whipped lightly

1 Lightly grease a baking tray.

2 Sift together the flour, salt, and baking powder into a mixing bowl. Stir in the sugar, then rub in the butter with your fingertips until the mixture resembles fine bread crumbs.

3 Pour in the milk and mix everything to a soft dough. On a lightly floured surface, knead the dough lightly, then roll out to a thickness of ½ inch.

Stamp out 4 rounds, using a 2-inch cutter. Transfer the rounds to the prepared baking sheet.

4 Bake in a preheated oven at 425°F for about 15 minutes, until the shortcakes are well risen and lightly browned. Let cool while you make the filling.

5 To make the filling, place the apple slices, sugar, lemon juice, and cinnamon in a saucepan.

6 Add the water, bring to a boil, and simmer uncovered for 5–10 minutes, until the apples are tender. Cool a little, then remove the apples from the pan.

7 To serve, split the shortcakes in half. Place each bottom half on an individual serving plate and spoon on a quarter of the apple slices, then the cream. Place the other half of the shortcake on top. Serve dusted with confectioners' sugar, if desired.

Orange Kugelhopf Cake

*Baking in a deep, fluted kugelhopf pan ensures that you create a cake
with a stunning shape. The moist cake is full of fresh orange flavor.*

Serves 6-8

INGREDIENTS

1 cup butter, softened
1 cup superfine sugar
4 eggs, separated
3³/₄ cups all-purpose flour
3 tsp baking powder
pinch of salt

1¹/₄ cups fresh orange juice
1 tbsp orange flower water
1 tsp grated orange rind

SYRUP:
³/₄ cup orange juice
1 cup granulated sugar

1 Grease and flour a 10 inch kugelhopf pan or deep ring mold.

2 In a bowl, cream together the butter and superfine sugar until light and fluffy. Add the egg yolks one at a time, whisking well after each addition.

3 Sift together the flour, salt, and baking powder into a separate bowl. Fold the dry ingredients and the orange juice alternately into the creamed mixture with a metal spoon, working as lightly as possible. Stir in the orange flower water, and orange rind.

4 Whisk the egg whites until they reach the soft peak stage and fold them into the mixture.

5 Pour into the prepared mold and bake in a preheated oven, 350°F, for 50-55 minutes or until a metal skewer inserted into the center of the cake comes out clean.

6 In a saucepan, bring the orange juice and sugar to a boil, then simmer for 5 minutes until the sugar has dissolved.

7 Remove the cake from the oven and leave to cool in the pan for 10 minutes. Prick the top of the cake with a fine skewer and brush over half of the syrup. Leave the cake to cool for another 10 minutes. Invert the cake on to a wire rack placed over a deep plate and brush the syrup over the cake until it is entirely covered. Serve.

Carrot Cake

*This classic favorite is always popular with children
and adults alike when it is served for afternoon tea.*

Makes 12 bars

INGREDIENTS

1 cup self-rising flour
pinch of salt
1 tsp ground cinnamon
$^3/_4$ cup soft brown sugar
2 eggs
scant $^1/_2$ cup sunflower oil
$4^1/_2$ oz carrot, peeled and grated
 finely

$^1/_3$ cup shredded coconut
$^1/_3$ cup walnuts, chopped
walnut pieces, for decoration

FROSTING:
10 tsp butter, softened
$1^3/_4$ oz full fat soft cheese
$1^1/_2$ cups confectioners' sugar, sifted
1 tsp lemon juice

1 Lightly grease a 8 inch square cake pan and line with baking parchment.

2 Sift the flour, salt, and ground cinnamon into a large bowl and stir in the brown sugar. Add the eggs and oil to the dry ingredients and mix well.

3 Stir in the grated carrot, shredded, coconut and chopped walnuts.

4 Pour the mixture into the prepared pan and bake in a preheated oven, 350°F, for 20-25 minutes or until just firm to the touch. Leave to cool in the pan.

5 Meanwhile, make the cheese frosting. In a bowl, beat together the butter, full fat soft cheese, confectioners' sugar and lemon juice until the mixture is fluffy and creamy.

6 Turn the cake out of the pan and cut into 12 bars or slices. Spread with the frosting and then decorate with walnut pieces.

VARIATION

*For a moister cake, replace
the coconut with 1 roughly
mashed banana.*

Lemon Syrup Cake

*The lovely light and tangy flavor of the sponge is balanced
by the lemony syrup poured over the top of the cake.*

Serves 8

INGREDIENTS

1³/₄ cups all-purpose flour
2 tsp baking powder
1 cup superfine sugar

4 eggs
²/₃ cup sour cream
grated rind 1 large lemon
4 tbsp lemon juice
²/₃ cup sunflower oil

SYRUP:
4 tbsp confectioners' sugar
3 tbsp lemon juice

1 Lightly grease a 8 inch loose-bottomed round cake pan and line the base with baking parchment.

2 Sift the flour and baking powder into a mixing bowl and stir in the sugar.

3 In a separate bowl, whisk the eggs, sour cream, lemon rind, lemon juice, and oil together.

4 Pour the egg mixture into the dry ingredients and mix well until evenly combined.

5 Pour the mixture into the prepared pan and bake in a preheated oven, 350°F, for 45-60 minutes until risen and golden brown.

6 Meanwhile, to make the syrup, mix together the confectioners' sugar and lemon juice in a small saucepan. Stir over a low heat until just beginning to bubble and turn syrupy.

7 As soon as the cake comes out of the oven prick the surface with a fine skewer, then brush the syrup over the top. Leave the cake to cool completely in the pan before turning out and serving.

COOK'S TIP

Pricking the surface of the hot cake with a skewer ensures that the syrup seeps right into the cake and the full flavor is absorbed.

Apple Cake with Cider

This can be eaten as a cake at tea time or with a cup of coffee, or it can be warmed through and served with cream for a dessert.

Makes a 8 inch cake

INGREDIENTS

2 cups self-rising flour
1 tsp baking powder
$^1/_3$ cup butter, cut into small pieces

$^1/_3$ cup superfine sugar
$1^3/_4$ oz dried apple, chopped
5 tbsp raisins

$^2/_3$ cup sweet cider
1 egg, beaten
6 oz raspberries

1 Grease a 8 inch cake pan and line it with baking parchment.

2 sift the flour and baking powder into a mixing bowl and rub in the butter with your fingers until the mixture resembles fine bread crumbs.

3 Stir in the superfine sugar, chopped dried apple, and raisins.

4 Pour in the sweet cider and egg and mix together until thoroughly blended. Stir in the raspberries very gently so they do not break up.

5 Pour the mixture into the prepared cake pan.

6 Bake in a preheated oven, 375°F, for about 40 minutes until risen and lightly golden.

7 Leave the cake to cool in the pan, then turn out on to a wire rack. Leave until completely cold before serving.

VARIATION

If you don't want to use cider, replace it with clear apple juice, if you prefer.

Olive Oil, Fruit, & Nut Cake

It is well worth using a good quality olive oil for this cake as this will determine its flavor. The cake will keep well in an airtight tin until ready to eat.

Serves 8

INGREDIENTS

2 cups self-rising flour
9 tsp superfine sugar

$^1/_2$ cup milk
4 tbsp orange juice
$^2/_3$ cup olive oil

$3^1/_2$ oz mixed dried fruit
1 oz pine nuts

1 Grease an 7 inch cake pan and line it with baking parchment.

2 sift the flour into a mixing bowl and stir in the superfine sugar.

3 Make a well in the center of the dry ingredients and pour in the milk and orange juice. Stir the mixture with a wooden spoon, beating in the flour and sugar.

4 Pour in the olive oil, stirring well so that all of the ingredients are evenly mixed.

5 Stir the mixed dried fruit and pine nuts into the mixture and spoon into the prepared pan.

6 Bake in a preheated oven, 350°F, for about 45 minutes until the cake is golden and firm to the touch.

7 Leave the cake to cool in the pan for a few minutes before transferring to a wire rack to cool.

8 Serve the cake warm or cold and cut into slices.

COOK'S TIP

Pine nuts are best known as the flavoring ingredient in the classic Italian pesto, but here they give a delicate, slightly resinous flavor to this cake.

Caraway Madeira

This is a classic Madeira cake made in the traditional way with caraway seeds. If you do not like their flavor, they can be omitted.

Serves 4

INGREDIENTS

1 cup butter, softened
1 cup soft brown sugar
3 eggs, beaten

3 cups self-rising flour
1 tbsp caraway seeds
grated rind of 1 lemon

6 tbsp milk
1 or 2 strips of citron peel

1 Grease and line a 2 lb loaf pan.

2 In a bowl, cream together the butter and soft brown sugar until pale and fluffy.

3 Gradually add the beaten eggs to the creamed mixture, beating well after each addition.

4 Sift the flour into the bowl and gently fold into the creamed mixture.

5 Add the caraway seeds, lemon rind, and the milk and fold in until thoroughly blended.

6 Spoon the mixture into the prepared pan and level the surface.

7 Bake in a preheated oven, 325°F, for 20 minutes.

8 Remove the cake from the oven, place the pieces of citron peel on top of the cake, and return it to the oven for a further 40 minutes or until the cake is well risen and a fine skewer inserted into the center comes out clean.

9 Leave the cake to cool in the pan before turning out and transferring to a wire rack until completely cold.

COOK'S TIP

Citron peel is available in the baking section of supermarkets. If it is unavailable, you can substitute it with chopped mixed peel.

Clementine Cake

This cake is flavored with clementine rind and juice, creating
a rich buttery cake but one full of fresh fruit flavor.

Serves 8

INGREDIENTS

2 clementines
3/4 cup butter, softened
3/4 cup superfine sugar
3 eggs, beaten

1 1/2 cups self-rising flour
3 tbsp ground almonds
3 tbsp light cream

GLAZE AND TOPPING:
6 tbsp clementine juice
2 tbsp superfine sugar
3 white sugar cubes, crushed

1 Grease an 7 inch round pan and line the base with baking parchment.

2 Pare the rind from the clementines and chop the rind finely. In a bowl, cream together the butter, sugar, and clementine rind until pale and fluffy.

3 Gradually add the beaten eggs to the mixture, beating well after each addition.

4 Gently fold in the self-rising flour followed by the ground almonds and the light cream. Spoon the mixture into the prepared pan.

5 Bake in a preheated oven, 350°F, for about 55-60 minutes or until a fine skewer inserted into the center comes out clean. Leave to cool slightly.

6 Meanwhile, make the glaze. Put the clementine juice into a small saucepan with the superfine sugar. Bring to a boil and simmer for 5 minutes.

7 Drizzle the glaze over the cake until it has been absorbed and sprinkle with the crushed sugar cubes.

COOK'S TIP

If you prefer, chop the rind from the clementines in a food processor or blender together with the sugar in step 2. Tip the mixture into a bowl with the butter and begin to cream the mixture.

Crunchy Fruit Cake

The cornmeal adds texture to this fruit cake, as well as an interesting golden yellow color. It also acts as a flour, binding the ingredients together to create a lighter texture.

Serves 8–10

INGREDIENTS

¹/₃ cup butter, softened
¹/₂ cup superfine sugar
2 eggs, beaten

¹/₃ cup self-rising flour, sifted
²/₃ cup cornmeal
1 tsp baking powder

8 oz mixed dried fruit
1oz pine nuts
grated rind of 1 lemon
4 tbsp lemon juice
2 tbsp milk

1 Grease an 7 inch cake pan and line the base with baking parchment.

2 In a bowl, whisk together the butter and sugar until light and fluffy.

3 Whisk in the beaten eggs a little at a time, whisking well after each addition.

4 Fold the flour, baking powder, and cornmeal into the mixture until well blended.

5 Stir in the mixed dried fruit, pine nuts, grated lemon rind, lemon juice, and milk.

6 Spoon the mixture into the prepared pan and level the surface.

7 Bake in a preheated oven, 350°F, for about 1 hour or until a fine skewer inserted into the center of the cake comes out clean.

8 Leave the cake to cool in the pan before turning out.

VARIATION

To give a more crumbly light fruit cake, omit the cornmeal and use 1 ¹/₄ cups self-rising flour instead.

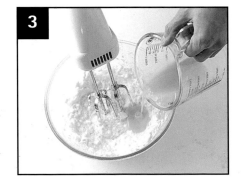

Candied Fruit Cake

This cake is extremely colorful; you can choose any mixture of candied fruits or stick to just one type if you prefer.

Serves 8

INGREDIENTS

$^3/_4$ cup butter, softened
$^3/_4$ cup superfine sugar
3 eggs, beaten

6 oz self-rising flour, sifted
1 oz ground rice
finely grated rind of 1 lemon

4 tbsp lemon juice
$^2/_3$ cup candied fruits, chopped
confectioners' sugar, for dusting
(optional)

1 Lightly grease an 7 inch cake pan and line with baking parchment.

2 In a bowl, whisk together the butter and superfine sugar until light and fluffy.

3 Add the beaten eggs a little at a time. Using a metal spoon, fold in the flour and ground rice.

4 Add the grated lemon rind and juice, followed by the chopped candied fruits. Lightly mix all the ingredients together.

5 Spoon the mixture into the prepared pan and level the surface with the back of a spoon or a knife.

6 Bake in a preheated oven, 350°F for 1-1 hour 10 minutes until well risen or until a fine skewer inserted into the center of the cake comes out clean.

7 Leave the cake to cool in the pan for 5 minutes, before turning it out on to a wire rack to cool completely.

8 Dust well with confectioners' sugar, if using, before serving.

COOK'S TIP

Wash and dry the candied fruits before chopping them. This will prevent the fruits sinking to the bottom of the cake during cooking.

White Chocolate & Apricot Squares

*The white chocolate makes this a very rich cake, so serve
it cut into small bars or squares or sliced thinly.*

Makes 12 bars

INGREDIENTS

¹/₂ cup butter
6 oz white chocolate, chopped
4 eggs

¹/₂ cup superfine sugar
1³/₄ cups all-purpose flour, sifted

1 tsp baking powder
pinch of salt
3¹/₂ oz ready-to-eat dried apricots,
 chopped

1 Lightly grease a 9 inch square cake pan and line the base smoothly with a sheet of baking parchment.

2 Melt the butter and chocolate in a heatproof bowl set over a saucepan of simmering water. Stir frequently with a wooden spoon until the mixture is smooth and glossy. Leave the mixture to cool slightly.

3 Beat the eggs and superfine sugar into the butter and chocolate mixture until well combined.

4 Fold in the flour, baking powder, salt, and chopped dried apricots and mix well.

5 Pour the mixture into the pan and bake in a preheated oven, 350°F, for 25-30 minutes.

6 The center of the cake may not be completely firm, but it will set as it cools. Leave in the pan to cool.

7 When the cake is completely cold turn it out and slice into bars or squares.

VARIATION

Replace the white chocolate with milk or dark chocolate, if you prefer.

Chocolate & Pear Sponge

What could be better than the lovely combination used in this cake of chocolate and fresh pears in a moist sponge.

Serves 6

INGREDIENTS

3/4 cup butter, softened
1 cup soft brown sugar
3 eggs, beaten

1 1/4 cups self-rising flour
2 tbsp cocoa powder

2 tbsp milk
2 small pears, peeled, cored, and sliced

1 Grease a 8 inch loose-bottomed cake pan and carefully line the base with baking parchment.

2 In a bowl, cream together the butter and soft brown sugar until pale and fluffy.

3 Gradually add the beaten eggs to the creamed mixture, beating well after each addition.

4 sift the self-rising flour and cocoa powder into the creamed mixture and fold in gently until all of the ingredients are combined.

5 Stir in the milk, then spoon the mixture into the prepared pan. Level the surface with the back of a spoon or a knife.

6 Arrange the pear slices on top of the cake mixture, arranging them in a radiating pattern.

7 Bake in a preheated oven, 350°F, for about 1 hour until the cake is just firm to the touch.

8 Leave the cake to cool in the pan, then transfer to a wire rack until completely cold before serving.

COOK'S TIP

Serve the cake with melted chocolate drizzled over the top for a delicious dessert.

Chocolate Slab Cake with Frosting

This chocolate slab cake gets its moist texture from the
sour cream which is stirred into the beaten mixture.

Serves 10–12

INGREDIENTS

1 cup butter

$3^1/_2$ oz dark chocolate, chopped

$^2/_3$ cup water

$2^1/_2$ cups all-purpose flour

2 tsp baking powder

$1^2/_3$ cups soft brown sugar

$^2/_3$ cup sour cream

2 eggs, beaten

FROSTING:

7 oz dark chocolate

6 tbsp water

3 tbsp light cream

1 tbsp butter, chilled

1 Grease a 33 x 13 x 8 inch square cake pan and line the bottom with baking parchment. In a saucepan, melt the butter and chocolate with the water over a low heat, stirring the mixture frequently.

2 sift the flour and baking powder into a mixing bowl and stir in the sugar.

3 Pour the hot chocolate liquid into the bowl and then beat well until all of the ingredients are evenly mixed. Stir in the sour cream, followed by the eggs.

4 Pour the mixture into the prepared pan and bake in a preheated oven, 375°F, for 40-45 minutes.

5 Leave the cake to cool in the pan before turning it out on to a wire rack. Leave it to cool completely.

6 To make the frosting, melt the chocolate with the water in a saucepan over a very low heat, stir in the cream and remove from the heat. Stir in the chilled butter, then pour the frosting over the cooled cake, using a spatula to spread it evenly over the top of the cake.

COOK'S TIP

Leave the cake on the wire rack to frost it and place a large baking sheet underneath to catch any drips.

Chocolate & Almond Torte

This torte is perfect for serving on a hot sunny day with heavy cream and a selection of fresh summer berries.

Serves 10

INGREDIENTS

8 oz dark chocolate, broken into pieces
3 tbsp water
1 cup soft brown sugar
3/4 cup butter, softened

1/4 cup ground almonds
3 tbsp self-rising flour
5 eggs, separated
1/4 cup blanched almonds, chopped finely

confectioners' sugar, for dusting
heavy cream, to serve (optional)

1 Grease a 9 inch loose-bottomed cake pan and base line with baking parchment.

2 In a saucepan set over a very low heat, melt the chocolate with the water, stirring until smooth. Add the sugar and stir until dissolved, taking the pan off the heat to prevent it overheating.

3 Add the butter in small amounts until it has melted into the chocolate. Remove from the heat and lightly stir in the ground almonds and flour. Add the egg yolks one at a time, beating well after each addition.

4 In a large mixing bowl, whisk the egg whites until they stand in soft peaks, then fold them into the chocolate mixture with a metal spoon. Stir in the chopped almonds. Pour the mixture into the pan and level the surface.

5 Bake in a preheated oven, 350°F, for 40-45 minutes until well risen and firm (the cake will crack on the surface during cooking).

6 Leave the cake to cool in the pan for 30-40 minutes, then turn it out on to a wire rack to cool completely. Dust with confectioners' sugar and serve in slices with heavy cream, if using.

COOK'S TIP

For a nuttier flavor, toast the chopped almonds in a dry skillet over a medium heat for about 2 minutes until lightly golden.

Chocolate & Raspberry Vacherin

A vacherin is made of layers of crisp meringue sandwiched together with fruit and cream. It makes a fabulous gateau for special occasions.

Serves 10–12

INGREDIENTS

3 egg whites
³/₄ cup superfine sugar
1 tsp cornstarch
1 oz dark chocolate, grated

FILLING:
6 oz dark chocolate
2 cups heavy cream, whipped

12 oz fresh raspberries
a little melted chocolate, to decorate

1 Draw 3 rectangles, 4 × 10 inches, on sheets of baking parchment and place on 2 baking cookie sheets.

2 Whisk the egg whites in a mixing bowl until standing in soft peaks, then gradually whisk in half of the sugar and continue whisking until the mixture is very stiff and glossy.

3 Carefully fold in the rest of the sugar, the cornstarch, and grated chocolate with a metal spoon or a spatula.

4 Spoon the meringue mixture into a pastry bag fitted with a ¹/₂ inch plain tip and pipe lines across the rectangles.

5 Bake in a preheated oven, 275°F, for 1¹/₂ hours, changing the positions of the baking sheets halfway through. Without opening the oven door, turn off the oven and leave the meringues to cool in the oven, then peel away the paper.

6 To make the filling, melt the chocolate and spread it over 2 of the meringue layers. Leave the filling to harden.

7 Place 1 chocolate-coated meringue on a plate and top with about one-third of the cream and raspberries. Gently place the second chocolate-coated meringue on top and spread with half of the remaining cream and raspberries.

8 Place the last meringue on the top and decorate it with the remaining cream and raspberries. Drizzle a little melted chocolate over the top and serve.

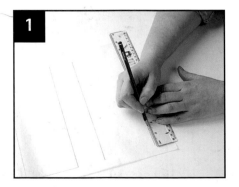

Chocolate Truffle Cake

Soft chocolatey sponge topped with a rich chocolate truffle mixture
makes a cake that chocoholics will die for.

Serves 12

INGREDIENTS

$^1/_3$ cup butter
$^1/_3$ cup superfine sugar
2 eggs, lightly beaten
$^2/_3$ cup self-rising flour
$^1/_2$ tsp baking powder
$^1/_4$ cup cocoa powder
$1^3/_4$ oz ground almonds

TRUFFLE TOPPING:
12 oz dark chocolate
$3^1/_2$ oz butter
$1^1/_4$ cups heavy cream
$1^1/_4$ cups plain cake crumbs
3 tbsp dark rum

TO DECORATE:
Cape gooseberries
$1^3/_4$ oz dark chocolate, melted

1 Lightly grease a 8 inch round springform pan and line the base. Beat together the butter and sugar until light and fluffy. Gradually add the eggs, beating well after each addition.

2 Sift the flour, baking powder, and cocoa powder together and fold into the mixture along with the ground almonds. Pour into the prepared pan and bake in a preheated oven, 350°F, for 20-25 minutes or until springy to the touch. Leave to cool slightly in the pan, then transfer to a wire rack to cool completely. Wash and dry the pan and return the cooled cake to the pan.

3 To make the topping, heat the chocolate, butter, and cream in a heavy-bottomed pan over a low heat and stir until smooth. Cool, then chill for 30 minutes. Beat well with a wooden spoon and chill for a further 30 minutes. Beat the mixture again, then add the cake crumbs and rum, beating until well combined. Spoon over the sponge base and chill for 3 hours.

4 Meanwhile, dip the Cape gooseberries in the melted chocolate until partially covered. Leave to set on baking parchment. Transfer the cake to a serving plate; decorate with Cape gooseberries.

White Chocolate Truffle Cake

A light white sponge, topped with a rich creamy-white chocolate truffle mixture makes an out-of-this-world gateau.

Serves 12

INGREDIENTS

2 eggs
4 tbsp superfine sugar
1/3 cup all-purpose flour
1 3/4 oz white chocolate, melted

TRUFFLE TOPPIING:
1 1/4 cups heavy cream
12 oz white chocolate, broken into pieces
9 oz Quark or fromage frais

TO DECORATE:
dark, milk, or white chocolate, melted
cocoa powder, to dust

1 Grease a 8 inch round springform pan and line the base. Whisk the eggs and superfine sugar in a mixing bowl for 10 minutes, or until the mixture is very light and foamy and the whisk leaves a trail that lasts a few seconds when lifted. Sift the flour and fold in with a metal spoon. Fold in the melted white chocolate. Pour into the pan and bake in a preheated oven, 350°F, for 25 minutes or until springy to the touch. Leave to cool slightly, then transfer to a wire rack until completely cold. Return the cold cake to the pan.

2 To make the topping, place the cream in a pan and bring to a boil, stirring to prevent it sticking to the bottom of the pan. Cool slightly, then add the white chocolate pieces and stir until melted and combined. Remove from the heat and leave until almost cool, stirring, then stir in the Quark or fromage frais. Pour the mixture on top of the cake and chill for 2 hours. Remove the cake from the pan and transfer to a serving plate.

3 To make large chocolate curls, pour melted chocolate on to a marble or acrylic board and spread it thinly with a palette spatula. Leave to set at room temperature. Using a scraper, push through the chocolate at a 25° angle until a large curl forms. Remove each curl as you make it and leave to chill until set. Decorate the cake with chocolate curls and sprinkle with a little cocoa powder.

Chocolate Almond Cake

Chocolate and almonds complement each other perfectly in this delicious cake.
Be warned, one slice will never be enough!

Serves 8–10

INGREDIENTS

6 oz dark chocolate
3/4 cup butter
4 1/2 oz superfine sugar
4 eggs, separated
1/4 tsp cream of tartar
1/3 cup self-rising flour

1 1/4 cups ground almonds
1 tsp almond extract

TOPPING:
4 1/2 oz milk chocolate
2 tbsp butter
4 tbsp heavy cream

TO DECORATE:
2 tbsp toasted slivered almonds
1 oz dark chocolate, melted

1 Lightly grease and line the base of a 9 inch round springform pan. Break the chocolate into small pieces and place in a small pan with the butter. Heat gently, stirring until melted and well combined.

2 Place 7 tbsp of the superfine sugar in a bowl with the egg yolks and whisk until pale and creamy. Add the melted chocolate mixture, beating until well combined.

3 sift the cream of tartar and flour together and fold into the chocolate mixture with the ground almonds and almond extract.

4 Whisk the egg whites in a bowl until standing in soft peaks. Add the remaining superfine sugar and whisk for about 2 minutes by hand, or 45-60 seconds, if using an electric whisk, until thick and glossy. Fold the egg whites into the chocolate mixture

and spoon into the pan. Bake in a preheated oven, 375°F, for 40 minutes until just springy to the touch. Let cool.

5 Heat the topping ingredients in a bowl over a pan of hot water. Remove from the heat and beat for 2 minutes. Let chill for 30 minutes. Transfer the cake to a plate and spread with the topping. Scatter with the almonds and drizzle with melted chocolate. Leave to set for 2 hours before serving.

Chocolate & Orange Cake

An all-time favorite combination of flavors means this cake is ideal for a tea-time treat.
Omit the frosting, if preferred, and sprinkle with confectioners' sugar.

Serves 8–10

INGREDIENTS

$^3/_4$ cup superfine sugar
$^3/_4$ cup butter or block margarine
3 eggs, beaten

1$^1/_2$ cups self-rising flour, sifted
2 tbsp cocoa powder, sifted

2 tbsp milk
3 tbsp orange juice
grated rind of $^1/_2$ orange

FROSTING:
1 cup confectioners' sugar
2 tbsp orange juice

1 Lightly grease a 8 inch deep round cake pan.

2 Beat together the sugar and butter or margarine in a bowl until light and fluffy. Gradually add the eggs, beating well after each addition. Carefully fold in the flour.

3 Divide the mixture in half. Add the cocoa powder and milk to one half, stirring until well combined. Flavor the other half with the orange juice and rind.

4 Place spoonfuls of each mixture into the prepared pan and swirl together with a skewer, to create a marbled effect. Bake in a preheated oven, 375°F, for 25 minutes or until springy to the touch.

5 Leave the cake to cool in the pan for a few minutes before transferring to a wire rack to cool completely.

6 To make the frosting, sift the confectioners' sugar into a mixing bowl and mix in enough of the orange juice to form a smooth frosting. Spread the frosting over the top of the cake and leave to set before serving.

VARIATION

Add 2 tablespoons of rum or brandy to the chocolate mixture instead of the milk. The cake also works well when flavored with grated lemon rind and juice instead of the orange.

Family Chocolate Cake

A simple to make family cake ideal for an everyday treat. Keep the decoration as simple as you like – you could use a bought frosting or filling, if liked.

Serves 8–10

INGREDIENTS

1/2 cup soft margarine
1/2 cup superfine sugar
2 eggs
1 tbsp light corn syrup
1 cup self-rising flour, sifted 2 tbsp
   cocoa powder, sifted

FILLING AND TOPPING:
1/4 cup confectioners' sugar, sifted
2 tbsp butter
3 1/2 oz white or milk cooking
   chocolate
a little milk or white chocolate,
   melted (optional)

1 Lightly grease two 7 inch shallow cake pans.

2 Place all of the ingredients for the cake in a large mixing bowl and beat with a wooden spoon or electric hand whisk to form a smooth mixture.

3 Divide the mixture between the prepared pans and level the tops. Bake in a preheated oven, 325F, for 20 minutes or until springy to the touch. Cool for a few minutes in the pans before transferring to a wire rack to cool completely.

4 To make the filling, beat the confectioners' sugar and butter together in a bowl until light and fluffy. Melt the cooking chocolate and beat half into the frosting mixture. Use the filling to sandwich the 2 cakes together.

5 Spread the remaining melted cooking chocolate over the top of the cake. Pipe circles of contrasting melted milk or white chocolate and feather into the cooking chocolate with a toothpick, if liked. Leave to set before serving.

COOK'S TIP

Ensure that you eat this cake on the day of baking, as it does not keep well.

Mocha Layer Cake

Chocolate cake and a creamy coffee-flavored filling
are combined in this delicious mocha cake.

Serves 8–10

INGREDIENTS

1 cup self-rising flour
$^1/_4$ tsp baking powder
4 tbsp cocoa powder
7 tbsp superfine sugar
2 eggs
2 tbsp light corn syrup
$^2/_3$ cup sunflower oil
$^2/_3$ cup milk

FILLING:
1 tsp instant coffee
1 tbsp boiling water
$1^1/_4$ cups heavy cream
2 tbsp confectioners' sugar

TO DECORATE:
$1^3/_4$ oz flock chocolate
chocolate caraque (see page 218)
confectioners' sugar, to dust

1 Lightly grease three 7 inch cake pans.

2 Sift the flour, baking powder, and cocoa powder into a large mixing bowl. Stir in the sugar. Make a well in the center and stir in the eggs, syrup, oil, and milk. Beat with a wooden spoon, gradually mixing in the dry ingredients to make a smooth batter. Divide the mixture between the prepared pans.

3 Bake in a preheated oven, 350°F, for 35-45 minutes or until springy to the touch. Leave in the pans for 5 minutes, then turn out on to a wire rack to cool completely.

4 Dissolve the instant coffee in the boiling water and place in a bowl with the cream and confectioners' sugar. Whip until the cream is just holding it's shape. Use half of the cream to sandwich the 3 cakes together. Spread the remaining cream over the top and sides of the cake. Lightly press the flock chocolate into the cream around the edge of the cake.

5 Transfer to a serving plate. Lay the caraque over the top of the cake. Cut a few thin strips of baking parchment and place on top of the caraque. Dust lightly with confectioners' sugar, then carefully remove the paper. Serve.

Rich Chocolate Layer Cake

Thin layers of delicious light chocolate cake sandwiched together with a rich chocolate frosting.

Serves 10–12

INGREDIENTS

7 eggs
1³/₄ cups superfine sugar
1¹/₄ cups all-purpose flour
¹/₂ cup cocoa powder
4 tbsp butter, melted

FILLING:
7 oz dark chocolate
¹/₂ cup butter
4 tbsp confectioners' sugar

TO DECORATE:
10 tbsp toasted slivered almonds,
    crushed lightly
small chocolate curls (see page 222)
    or grated chocolate

1 Grease a deep 9 inch square cake pan and line the base with baking parchment.

2 Whisk the eggs and superfine sugar in a mixing bowl with an electric whisk for about 10 minutes, or until the mixture is very light and foamy and the whisk leaves a trail that lasts a few seconds when lifted.

3 Sift the flour and cocoa together and fold half into the mixture. Drizzle over the melted butter and fold in the rest of the flour and cocoa. Pour into the prepared pan and bake in a preheated oven, 350°F, for 30–35 minutes or until springy to the touch. Leave to cool slightly, then remove from the pan and cool completely on a wire rack. Wash and dry the pan and return the cake to it.

4 To make the filling, melt the chocolate and butter together, then remove from the heat. Stir in the confectioners' sugar, leave to cool, then beat until thick enough to spread.

5 Halve the cake lengthways and cut each half into 3 layers. Sandwich the layers together with three-quarters of the chocolate filling. Spread the remainder over the cake and mark a wavy pattern on the top. Press the almonds on to the sides. Decorate with chocolate curls or grated chocolate.

Devil's Food Cake

This is an classic, consisting of a rich melt-in-the-mouth chocolate cake that has a citrus-flavored frosting.

Serves 8

INGREDIENTS

3^1/$_2$ oz dark chocolate
2^1/$_4$ cups self-rising flour
1 tsp baking soda
1 cup butter

2^2/$_3$ cups dark muscovado sugar
1 tsp vanilla extract

3 eggs
^{1}/$_2$ cup buttermilk
2 cups boiling water

FROSTING:
1^1/$_3$ cups superfine sugar
2 egg whites

1 tbsp lemon juice
3 tbsp orange juice
candied orange peel, to decorate

1 Lightly grease two 8 inch shallow round cake pans and line the bases. Melt the chocolate in a pan. sift the flour and baking soda together.

2 Beat the butter and sugar in a bowl until pale and fluffy. Beat in the vanilla extract and the eggs, one at a time and beating well after each addition. Add a little flour if the mixture begins to curdle.

3 Fold the melted chocolate into the mixture until well blended. Gradually fold in the remaining flour, then stir in the buttermilk and boiling water.

4 Divide the mixture between the pans and level the tops. Bake in a preheated oven, 375°F, for 30 minutes until springy to the touch. Leave to cool in the pan for 5 minutes, then transfer to a wire rack to cool completely.

5 Place the frosting ingredients in a large bowl set over a pan of gently simmering water. Whisk, preferably with an electric beater, until thickened and forming soft peaks. Remove from the heat and whisk until the mixture is cool.

6 Sandwich the 2 cakes together with a little of the frosting, then spread the remainder over the sides and top of the cake, swirling it as you do so. Decorate with the candied orange peel.

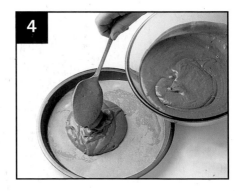

Chocolate Yogurt Cake

*Adding yogurt to the cake mixture gives the baked
cake a deliciously moist texture.*

Serves 8-10

INGREDIENTS

$^2/_3$ cup vegetable oil
$^2/_3$ cup whole milk unsweetened
   yogurt
$1^1/_4$ cups light muscovado sugar
3 eggs, beaten
$^3/_4$ cup whole wheat self-rising flour
1 cup self-rising flour, sifted
2 tbsp cocoa powder

1 tsp baking soda
$1^3/_4$ oz dark chocolate, melted

FILLING AND TOPPING:
$^2/_3$ cup whole milk unsweetened
   yogurt
$^2/_3$ cup heavy cream
8 oz fresh soft fruit, such as
   strawberries or raspberries

1 Grease a deep 9 inch round cake pan and line the base with baking parchment.

2 Place the oil, yogurt, sugar, and beaten eggs in a large mixing bowl and beat together until well combined. sift the flours, cocoa powder, and baking soda together and beat into the bowl until well combined. Beat in the melted chocolate.

3 Pour into the prepared pan and bake in a preheated oven, 350°F, for 45-50 minutes or until a fine skewer inserted into the center comes out clean. Leave to cool in the pan for 5 minutes, then turn out on to a wire rack to cool completely. When cold, split the cake into 3 layers.

4 To make the filling, place the yogurt and cream in a large mixing bowl and whisk well until the mixture stands in soft peaks.

5 Place one layer of cake on to a serving plate and spread with some of the cream. Top with a little of the fruit (slicing larger fruit such as strawberries). Repeat with the next layer. Top with the final layer of cake and spread with the rest of the cream. Arrange more fruit on top and cut the cake into wedges to serve.

Chocolate Passion Cake

What could be nicer than passion cake with added chocolate?
Rich and moist, this cake is fabulous with afternoon tea.

Serves 10–12

INGREDIENTS

5 eggs
²/₃ cup superfine sugar
1¹/₄ cups all-purpose flour

¹/₃ cup cocoa powder
6 oz carrots, peeled and finely grated
¹/₂ cup chopped walnuts
2 tbsp sunflower oil

12 oz medium fat soft cheese
1 cup confectioners' sugar
6 oz milk or dark chocolate, melted

1 Lightly grease and line the base of a 8 inch deep round cake pan.

2 Place the eggs and sugar in a large mixing bowl set over a pan of gently simmering water and whisk until very thick. Lift the whisk up and let the mixture drizzle back – it will leave a trail for a few seconds when thick enough.

3 Remove the bowl from the heat. sift the flour and cocoa powder into the bowl and fold in carefully. Then fold in the carrots, walnuts, and oil until just combined.

4 Pour into the prepared pan and bake in a preheated oven, 375°F, for 45 minutes or until well risen and springy to the touch. Leave to cool slightly then turn out on to a wire rack to cool completely.

5 Beat together the soft cheese and confectioners' sugar until combined. Beat in the melted chocolate. Split the cake in half and sandwich together again with half of the chocolate mixture. Cover the top of the cake with the remainder of the chocolate mixture, swirling it with a knife. Leave to chill or serve at once.

COOK'S TIP

The undecorated cake can be frozen for up to 2 months. Defrost at room temperature for 3 hours or overnight in the refrigerator.

Chocolate & Orange Mousse Cake

With a dark chocolate sponge sandwiched together with a light creamy
orange mousse, this spectacular cake is irresistible.

Serves 12

INGREDIENTS

³/₄ cup butter
³/₄ cup superfine sugar
4 eggs, lightly beaten
1³/₄ cups self-rising flour
1 tbsp cocoa powder
1³/₄ oz dark orange-flavored
  chocolate, melted

ORANGE MOUSSE:
2 eggs, separated
4 tbsp superfine sugar
³/₄ cup freshly squeezed orange juice
2 tsp gelatine
3 tbsp water
1¹/₄ cups heavy cream

peeled orange slices, to decorate

1 Grease a 8 inch springform cake pan and and line the base. Beat the butter and sugar in a bowl until light and fluffy. Gradually add the eggs, beating well after each addition. sift together the cocoa and flour and fold into the cake mixture. Fold in the chocolate.

2 Pour into the prepared pan and level the top. Bake in a preheated oven, 350°F, for 40 minutes or until springy to the touch. Leave to cool for 5 minutes in the pan, then turn out and leave to cool completely on a wire rack. Cut the cold cake into 2 layers.

3 To make the orange mousse, beat the egg yolks and sugar until light, then whisk in the orange juice. Sprinkle the gelatine over the water in a small bowl and allow to go spongy, then place over a pan of hot water and stir until dissolved. Stir into the mousse.

4 Whip the cream until holding its shape, reserve a little for decoration, and fold the rest into the mousse. Whisk the egg whites until standing in soft peaks, then fold in. Leave in a cool place until starting to set, stirring occasionally.

5 Place half of the cake in the pan. Pour in the mousse and press the second cake layer on top. Chill until set. Transfer to a dish, pipe cream rosettes on the top, and arrange orange slices in the center.

Chocolate & Vanilla Loaf Cake

*An old-fashioned favorite, this cake will keep well if stored
in an airtight container or wrapped in foil in a cool place.*

Serves 10

INGREDIENTS

³/₄ cup superfine sugar
³/₄ cup soft margarine
¹/₂ tsp vanilla extract
3 eggs

2 cups self-rising flour, sifted
1³/₄ oz dark chocolate
confectioners' sugar, to dust

1 Lightly grease a 1 lb loaf pan.

2 Beat together the sugar and soft margarine in a bowl until light and fluffy.

3 Beat in the vanilla extract. Gradually add the eggs, beating well after each addition. Carefully fold in the self-rising flour.

4 Divide the mixture in half. Melt the dark chocolate and stir into one half of the mixture until well combined.

5 Place the vanilla mixture in the pan and level the top. Spread the chocolate layer over the vanilla layer.

6 Bake in a preheated oven, 375°F, for 30 minutes or until springy to the touch.

7 Leave to cool in the pan before transferring the loaf to a wire rack to cool completely.

8 Serve the cake dusted with confectioners' sugar.

COOK'S TIP

Freeze the cake undecorated for up to 2 months. Defrost at room temperature.

VARIATION

If liked, the mixtures can be marbled together with a toothpick.

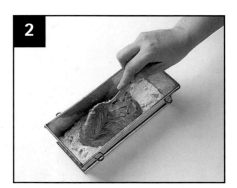

Chocolate & Walnut Cake

This walnut-studded chocolate cake has a tasty chocolate butter frosting. It is perfect for serving at coffee mornings as it can easily be made the day before.

Serves 8–12

INGREDIENTS

4 eggs
$^{1}/_{2}$ cup superfine sugar
1 cup all-purpose flour
1 tbsp cocoa powder
2 tbsp butter, melted
$2^{3}/_{4}$ oz dark chocolate, melted
$1^{1}/_{4}$ cups finely chopped walnuts

FROSTING:
$2^{3}/_{4}$ oz dark chocolate
$^{1}/_{2}$ cup butter
$1^{1}/_{4}$ cups confectioners' sugar
2 tbsp milk
walnut halves, to decorate

1 Grease a 7 inch deep round cake pan and line the base. Place the eggs and superfine sugar in a mixing bowl and whisk with electric beaters for 10 minutes, or until the mixture is light and foamy and the whisk leaves a trail that lasts a few seconds when lifted.

2 Sift together the flour and cocoa powder and fold in with a metal spoon or spatula. Fold in the melted butter and chocolate, and the chopped walnuts. Pour into the prepared pan and bake in a preheated oven, 325°F, and bake for 30–35 minutes or until springy to the touch.

3 Leave to cool in the pan for 5 minutes, then transfer to a wire rack to cool completely. Cut the cold cake into 2 layers.

4 To make the frosting, melt the dark chocolate and leave to cool slightly. Beat together the butter, confectioners' sugar, and milk in a bowl until the mixture is pale and fluffy. Whisk in the melted chocolate.

5 Sandwich the 2 cake layers with some of the frosting and place on a serving plate. Spread the remaining frosting over the top of the cake with a spatula, swirling it slightly as you do so. Decorate the cake with the walnut halves and serve.

Chocolate Lamington Bar Cake

*This cake is based on the famous Australian Lamington cake, named after Lord Lamington,
a former Governor of Queensland, which has chocolate frosting covered with coconut.*

Serves 8-10

INGREDIENTS

³/₄ cup butter or block margarine
³/₄ cup superfine sugar
3 eggs, lightly beaten
1¹/₄ cups self-rising flour
2 tbsp cocoa powder
³/₄ cup confectioners' sugar

1³/₄ oz dark chocolate, broken into
  pieces
5 tbsp milk
1 tsp butter
about 8 tbsp shredded coconut
¹/₄ pint heavy cream, whipped

1 Lightly grease a 1 lb loaf pan – preferably a long, thin pan about 3 × 10 inches.

2 Cream together the butter and sugar in a bowl until light and fluffy. Gradually add the eggs, beating well after each addition. sift together the flour and cocoa. Fold into the mixture.

3 Pour the mixture into the prepared pan and level the top. Bake in a preheated oven, 350°F, for 40 minutes or until springy to the touch. Leave to cool for 5 minutes in the pan, then turn out on to a wire rack to cool completely.

4 Place the chocolate, milk, and butter in a heatproof bowl set over a pan of hot water. Stir until the chocolate has melted. Add the confectioners' sugar and beat until smooth. Leave to cool until the frosting is thick enough to spread, then spread it all over the cake.

Sprinkle with the coconut and allow the frosting to set.

5 Cut a V-shape wedge from the top of the cake. Put the cream in a pastry bag fitted with a plain or star tip. Pipe the cream down the center of the wedge and replace the wedge of cake on top of the cream. Pipe another line of cream down either side of the wedge of cake. Serve.

Chocolate Ganache Cake

Ganache – a divine mixture of chocolate and cream – is used to fill and decorate this rich chocolate cake, making it a chocolate lover's dream.

Serves 10–12

INGREDIENTS

3/4 cup butter
3/4 cup superfine sugar
4 eggs, lightly beaten
1 3/4 cups self-rising flour
1 tbsp cocoa powder
1 3/4 oz dark chocolate, melted

GANACHE:
2 cups heavy cream
13 oz dark chocolate, broken into
  pieces

TO FINISH:
7 oz chocolate-flavored cake
  covering

1 Lightly grease a 8 inch springform cake pan and line the base. Beat the butter and sugar until light and fluffy. Gradually add the eggs, beating well after each addition. sift together the flour and cocoa. Fold into the cake mixture. Fold in the melted chocolate.

2 Pour into the prepared pan and level the top. Bake in a preheated oven, 350°F, for 40 minutes or until springy to the touch. Leave to cool for 5 minutes in the pan, then turn out on to a wire rack and leave to cool completely. Cut the cold cake into 2 layers.

3 To make the ganache, place the cream in a pan and bring to a boil, stirring. Add the chocolate and stir until melted and combined. Pour into a bowl and whisk for about 5 minutes or until the ganache is fluffy and cool.

4 Reserve one-third of the ganache. Use the remaining ganache to sandwich the cake together and spread over the top and sides of the cake.

5 Melt the cake covering and spread it over a large sheet of baking parchment. Cool until just set. Cut into strips a little wider than the height of the cake. Place the strips around the edge of the cake, overlapping them slightly.

6 Pipe the reserved ganache in tear drop or shells to cover the top of the cake. Chill for 1 hour.

Chocolate & Mango Layer

Peaches can be used instead of mangoes for this deliciously moist cake, if you prefer. If the top of the cake is very domed, cut a piece off, then turn the cake upside down so that you have a flat surface to decorate.

Serves 12

INGREDIENTS

$1/2$ cup cocoa powder
$2/3$ cup boiling water
6 large eggs
$1^1/2$ cups superfine sugar
$2^1/2$ cups self-rising flour

2 x 14 oz cans mango
1 tsp cornstarch

generous $1^3/4$ cups heavy cream
$2^3/4$ oz dark flock chocolate or grated chocolate

1 Grease a deep 9 inch round cake pan and line the base with baking parchment.

2 Place the cocoa powder in a small bowl and gradually add the boiling water; blend to form a smooth paste.

3 Place the eggs and superfine sugar in a mixing bowl and whisk until the mixture is very light and foamy and the whisk leaves a trail that lasts a few seconds when lifted. Fold in the cocoa mixture. Sift the flour and fold into the mixture.

4 Pour the mixture into the pan and level the top. Bake in a preheated oven, 325°F, for about 1 hour or until springy to the touch.

5 Leave to cool in the pan for a few minutes then turn out and cool completely on a wire rack. Peel off the lining paper and cut the cake into 3 layers.

6 Drain the mangoes and place a quarter of them in a food processor and purée until smooth. Mix the cornstarch with about 3 tbsp of the mango juice to form a smooth paste. Add to the mango

purée. Transfer to a small pan and heat gently, stirring until the purée thickens. Leave to cool.

7 Chop the remaining mango. Whip the cream and reserve about one quarter. Fold the mango into the remaining cream and use to sandwich the layers of cake together. Place on a serving plate. Spread some of the remaining cream around the side of the cake. Press the flock or grated chocolate lightly into the cream. Pipe cream rosettes around the top. Spread the mango purée over the center.

Chocolate Layer Log

*This unusual cake is very popular with children who love
the appearance of the layers when it is sliced.*

Serves 8–10

INGREDIENTS

¹/₂ cup soft margarine
¹/₂ cup superfine sugar
2 eggs
³/₄ cup self-rising flour
¹/₄ cup cocoa powder
2 tbsp milk

WHITE CHOCOLATE BUTTER CREAM:
2³/₄ oz white chocolate
2 tbsp milk
²/₃ cup butter
³/₄ cup confectioners' sugar
2 tbsp orange-flavored liqueur

large dark chocolate curls (see page 50), to decorate

1 Grease and line the sides of two 14 oz food cans.

2 Beat together the margarine and sugar in a bowl until light and fluffy. Gradually add the eggs, beating well after each addition. sift together the flour and cocoa powder and fold into the cake mixture. Fold in the milk.

3 Divide the mixture between the two prepared cans. Stand the cans on a baking cookie sheet and bake in a preheated oven, 350°F, for 40 minutes or until springy to the touch. Leave to cool for about 5 minutes in the cans, then turn out and leave to cool completely on a wire rack.

4 To make the butter cream, put the chocolate and milk in a pan and heat gently until the chocolate has melted, stirring until well combined. Leave to cool slightly. Beat together the butter and confectioners' sugar until light and fluffy. Beat in the orange liqueur. Gradually beat in the chocolate mixture.

5 To assemble, cut both cakes into ¹/₂ inch thick slices, then reassemble them by sandwiching the slices together with some of the butter cream.

6 Place the cake on a serving plate and spread the remaining butter cream over the top and sides. Decorate with the chocolate curls, then serve the cake cut diagonally into slices.

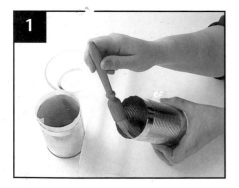

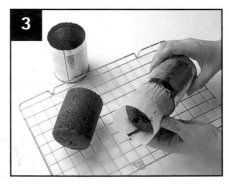

Chocolate Roulade

Don't worry if the cake cracks when rolled, this is quite normal. If it doesn't crack, you can consider yourself a real chocolate wizard in the kitchen!

Serves 6-8

INGREDIENTS

5^1/$_2$ oz dark chocolate
2 tbsp water
6 eggs
^{3}/$_4$ cup superfine sugar
^{1}/$_4$ cup all-purpose flour
1 tbsp cocoa powder

FILLING:
1^1/$_4$ cups heavy cream
2^3/$_4$ oz sliced strawberries

TO DECORATE:
confectioners' sugar
chocolate leaves (see below)

1 Line a 15 × 10 inch pan. Melt the chocolate in the water, stirring. Leave to cool slightly.

2 Place the eggs and sugar in a bowl and whisk for 10 minutes, or until the mixture is pale and foamy and the whisk leaves a trail when lifted. Whisk in the chocolate in a thin stream. Sift the flour and cocoa together and fold into the mixture. Pour into the pan; level the top.

3 Bake in a preheated oven, 400°F, for 12 minutes. Dust a sheet of baking parchment with a little confectioners' sugar. Turn out the roulade and remove the lining paper. Roll up the roulade with the fresh parchment inside. Place on a wire rack, cover, with a damp dish cloth and leave to cool.

4 Whisk the cream until just holding its shape. Unroll the roulade and scatter over the fruit. Spread three-quarters of the cream over the roulade and re-roll. Dust with confectioners' sugar. Place the roulade on a plate. Pipe the rest of the cream down the center and decorate with chocolate leaves.

5 To make chocolate leaves, wash some rose or holly leaves and pat dry. Melt some chocolate and brush over the leaves. Set aside to harden. Repeat with 2-3 layers of chocolate. Carefully peel the leaves away from the chocolate.

Chocolate & Coconut Roulade

A coconut-flavored roulade is encased in a rich chocolate coating. A fresh
raspberry coulis gives a lovely fresh contrast to the sweetness of the roulade.

Serves 8–10

INGREDIENTS

3 eggs
$1/3$ cup superfine sugar
$1/3$ cup self-rising flour
1 tbsp block creamed coconut,
  softened with 1 tbsp boiling water
1 oz shredded coconut
6 tbsp good raspberry conserve

CHOCOLATE COATING:
7 oz dark chocolate
$1/4$ cup butter
2 tbsp light corn syrup

RASPBERRY COULIS:
8 oz fresh or frozen raspberries,
  thawed if frozen
2 tbsp water
4 tbsp confectioners' sugar

1 Grease and line a 9 × 12 inch pan. Whisk the eggs and superfine sugar in a large mixing bowl with electric beaters for about 10 minutes or until the mixture is very light and foamy and the whisk leaves a trail that lasts a few seconds when lifted.

2 Sift the flour and fold in with a metal spoon or a spatula. Fold in the creamed coconut and shredded coconut. Pour into the prepared pan and bake in a preheated oven, 400°F, for 10-12 minutes, or until springy to the touch.

3 Sprinkle a sheet of baking parchment with a little superfine sugar and place on top of a damp dish cloth. Turn the cake out on to the paper and carefully peel away the lining paper. Spread the jam over the sponge and roll up from the short end, using the tea towel to help you. Place seam-side down on a wire rack and leave to cool completely.

4 To make the coating, melt the chocolate and butter, stirring. Stir in the light corn syrup; leave to cool for 5 minutes. Spread it over the roulade and leave to set. To make the coulis, purée the fruit in a food processor with the water and sugar; sift to remove the seeds. Cut the roulade into slices and serve with the coulis.

Dark & White Chocolate Torte

If you can not decide if you prefer bitter dark chocolate or rich creamy white chocolate then this gateau is for you.

Serves 10

INGREDIENTS

4 eggs
7 tbsp cup superfine sugar
³/₄ cup all-purpose flour

DARK CHOCOLATE CREAM:
²/₃ cup heavy cream

5¹/₂ oz dark chocolate, broken into
  small pieces

WHITE CHOCOLATE FROSTING:
2³/₄ oz white chocolate
1 tbsp butter

1 tbsp milk
4 tbsp confectioners' sugar
chocolate caraque (see page 218)

1 Grease a 8 inch round springform pan and line the base. Whisk the eggs and superfine sugar in a large mixing bowl with electric beaters for about 10 minutes, or until the mixture is very light and foamy and the whisk leaves a trail that lasts a few seconds when lifted.

2 Sift the flour and fold in with a metal spoon or spatula. Pour into the prepared pan and bake in a preheated oven, 350°F,

for 35-40 minutes, or until springy to the touch. Leave to cool slightly, then transfer to a wire rack to cool completely. Cut the cold cake into 2 layers.

3 To make the chocolate cream, place the cream in a saucepan and bring to a boil, stirring. Add the chocolate and stir until melted and well combined. Remove from the heat and leave to cool. Beat with a wooden spoon until thick.

4 Sandwich the 2 cake layers back together with the chocolate cream and place on a wire rack.

5 To make the frosting, melt the chocolate and butter together and stir until blended. Whisk in the milk and confectioners' sugar. Whisk for a few minutes until the frosting is cool. Pour it over the cake and spread with a spatula to coat the top and sides. Decorate with chocolate caraque and leave to set.

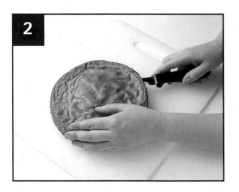

Sachertorte

This rich melt-in-the mouth cake originates in Austria. Make sure you have a steady hand when writing the name on the top. If preferred, you could drizzle a random scribble of chocolate instead.

Serves 10-12

INGREDIENTS

6 oz dark chocolate
²/₃ cup unsalted butter
²/₃ cup superfine sugar
6 eggs, separated
1¹/₄ cups all-purpose flour

FROSTING AND FILLING:
6 oz dark chocolate
5 tbsp strong black coffee
1 cup confectioners' sugar

6 tbsp good apricot preserve
1³/₄ oz dark chocolate, melted

1 Grease a 9 inch springform cake pan and line the base. Melt the chocolate. Beat the butter and ¹/₃ cup of the sugar until pale and fluffy. Add the egg yolks and beat well. Add the chocolate in a thin stream, beating well. Sift the flour; fold it into the mixture. Whisk the egg whites until they stand in soft peaks. Add the remaining sugar and whisk for 2 minutes by hand, or 45-60 seconds if using an electric whisk, until glossy. Fold half into the chocolate mixture, then fold in the remainder.

2 Spoon into the prepared pan and level the top. Bake in a preheated oven, 300°F, for 1-1¹/₄ hours until a skewer inserted into the center comes out clean. Cool in the pan for 5 minutes, then transfer to a wire rack to cool completely.

3 To make the frosting, melt the chocolate and beat in the coffee until smooth. Sift the confectioners' sugar into a bowl. Whisk in the melted chocolate mixture to give a thick frosting. Halve the cake. Warm the jam,

spread over one half of the cake and sandwich together. Invert the cake on a wire rack. Spoon the frosting over the cake and spread to coat the top and sides. Leave to set for 5 minutes, allowing any excess frosting to drop through the rack. Transfer to a serving plate and leave to set for at least 2 hours.

4 To decorate, spoon the melted chocolate into a small pastry bag and pipe the word 'Sacher' or 'Sachertorte' on the top of the cake. Leave it to harden before serving the cake.

Bistvitny Torte

This is a Russian marbled chocolate cake that is soaked in a delicious flavored syrup and decorated with chocolate and cream.

Serves 10

INGREDIENTS

CHOCOLATE TRIANGLES:
1 oz dark chocolate, melted
1 oz white chocolate, melted

CAKE:
$^3/_4$ cup soft margarine

$^3/_4$ cup superfine sugar
$^1/_2$ tsp vanilla extract
3 eggs, lightly beaten
2 cups self-rising flour
$1^3/_4$ oz dark chocolate

SYRUP:
$^1/_2$ cup sugar
6 tbsp water
3 tbsp brandy or sherry
$1^2/_3$ cup heavy cream

1 Grease a 9 inch ring pan. To make the triangles, place a sheet of baking parchment on to a baking sheet and place alternate spoonfuls of the dark and white chocolate on to the paper. Spread together to form a thick marbled layer; leave to set. Cut into squares, then into triangles.

2 To make the cake, beat the margarine and sugar until light and fluffy. Beat in the vanilla extract. Gradually add the eggs, beating well after each addition.

Fold in the flour. Divide the mixture in half. Melt the dark chocolate and stir into one half.

3 Place spoonfuls of each mixture into the prepared pan and swirl together with a skewer to create a marbled effect.

4 Bake in a preheated oven, 375°F, for 30 minutes, or until the cake is springy to the touch. Leave it to cool in the pan for a few minutes, then transfer to a wire rack to cool completely.

5 To make the syrup, place the sugar in a small pan with the water and heat until the sugar has dissolved. Boil for 1-2 minutes. Remove from the heat and stir in the brandy or sherry. Leave the syrup to cool slightly then spoon it slowly over the cake, allowing it to soak into the sponge. Whip the cream and pipe swirls of it on top of the cake. Decorate with the chocolate triangles.

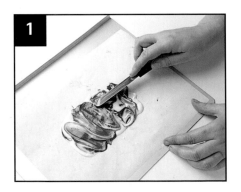

Dobos Torte

This wonderful cake originates from Hungary and consists of thin layers of light sponge sandwiched together with butter cream and topped with a crunchy caramel layer.

Serves 8

INGREDIENTS

3 eggs
7 tbsp superfine sugar
1 tsp vanilla extract
$^1/_2$ cup all-purpose flour

FILLING:
6 oz dark chocolate
$^3/_4$ cup butter
2 tbsp milk
2 cups confectioners' sugar

CARAMEL:
7 tbsp granulated sugar
4 tbsp water

1 Draw four 7 inch circles on sheets of baking parchment. Place 2 of them upside down on 2 baking sheets. Whisk the eggs and superfine sugar in a large mixing bowl with electric beaters for 10 minutes, or until the mixture is light and foamy and the whisk leaves a trail. Fold in the vanilla extract. Sift the flour and fold in with a metal spoon or a spatula. Spoon a quarter of the mixture on to one of the sheets and spread out to the size of the circle. Repeat with the other circle. Bake in a preheated oven, 400°F, for 5-8 minutes or until golden brown. Cool on wire racks. Repeat with the remaining mixture.

2 To make the filling, melt the chocolate and cool slightly. Beat the butter, milk, and confectioners' sugar until pale and fluffy. Whisk in the chocolate. Place the sugar and water for the caramel in a heavy-bottomed pan and heat gently, stirring until the sugar dissolves. Boil gently until the syrup is pale golden. Remove from the heat. Pour over one layer of the cake to cover the top. Leave to harden slightly, then mark into 8 portions with an oiled knife. Remove the cakes from the paper and trim the edges. Sandwich the layers together with some of the filling, finishing with the caramel-topped cake. Place on a serving plate and spread the sides with the filling mixture, using a comb scraper if you have one. Pipe rosettes around the top of the cake.

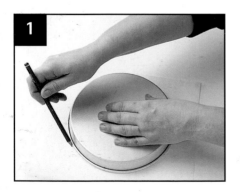

Bûche de Noël

This is the traditional French Christmas cake. It consists of a chocolate cake filled and encased in a delicious rich chocolate frosting.

Serves 8–10

INGREDIENTS

CAKE:
4 eggs
7 tbsp superfine sugar
$^2/_3$ cup self-rising flour
2 tbsp cocoa powder

FROSTING:
$5^1/_2$ oz dark chocolate
2 egg yolks
$^2/_3$ cup milk
$^1/_2$ cup butter
4 tbsp confectioners' sugar
2 tbsp rum (optional)

TO DECORATE:
a little white glacé or royal frosting
confectioners' sugar, to dust
holly or Christmas cake decorations

1 Grease and line a 12 × 9 inch pan. Whisk the eggs and superfine sugar in a bowl with electric beaters for 10 minutes, or until the mixture is very light and foamy and the whisk leaves a trail. sift the flour and cocoa powder and fold in. Pour into the prepared pan and bake in a preheated oven, 400°F, for 12 minutes or until springy to the touch. Turn out on to a piece of baking parchment which has been sprinkled with a little superfine sugar. Peel off the lining paper and trim the edges. Cut a small slit halfway into the cake about $^1/_2$ inch from one short end. Starting at that end, roll up tightly, enclosing the paper. Place on a wire rack to cool.

2 To make the frosting, break the chocolate into pieces and melt it over a pan of hot water. Beat in the egg yolks, whisk in the milk and cook until the mixture thickens enough to coat the back of a wooden spoon, stirring. Cover with dampened greaseproof paper and cool. Beat the butter and sugar until pale and fluffy. Beat in the custard and rum, if using. Unroll the sponge, spread with one-third of the frosting and roll up again. Place on a serving plate. Spread the remaining frosting over the cake and mark with a fork to give the effect of bark. Leave to set. Pipe white frosting to form the rings of the log. Sprinkle with sugar and decorate.

Low-Fat Chocolate & Pineapple Cake

Decorated with thick yogurt and canned pineapple, this is a low-fat cake, but it is by no means lacking in flavor.

Serves 9

INGREDIENTS

$^2/_3$ cup low-fat spread
$4^1/_2$ oz superfine sugar
$^3/_4$ cup self-rising flour, sifted
3 tbsp cocoa powder, sifted

$1^1/_2$ tsp baking powder
2 eggs
8 oz can pineapple pieces in unsweetened juice

$^1/_2$ cup low-fat thick unsweetened yogurt
about 1 tbsp confectioners' sugar
grated chocolate, to decorate

1 Lightly grease a 8 inch square cake pan.

2 Place the low-fat spread, superfine sugar, flour, cocoa powder, baking powder, and eggs in a large mixing bowl. Beat with a wooden spoon or electric hand whisk until smooth.

3 Pour the cake mixture into the prepared pan and level the surface. Bake it in a preheated oven, 325°F, for 20-25 minutes or until springy to the touch. Leave the cake to cool slightly in the pan before transferring to a wire rack to cool completely.

4 Drain the pineapple, chop the pineapple pieces, and drain again. Reserve a little pineapple for decoration, then stir the rest into the yogurt and sweeten to taste with confectioners' sugar.

5 Spread the pineapple and yogurt mixture over the cake and decorate with the reserved pineapple pieces. Sprinkle with the grated chocolate.

COOK'S TIP

Store the cake, undecorated, in an airtight container for up to 3 days. Once decorated, refrigerate and use within 2 days.

Sugar-Free Fruit Cake

*This cake is full of flavor from the mixed fruits. The fruit gives
the cake its sweetness so there is no need for extra sugar.*

Serves 8-10

INGREDIENTS

3 cups all-purpose flour

2 tsp baking powder

1 tsp ground allspice

1/2 cup butter, cut into small pieces

2 3/4 oz ready-to-eat dried apricots,
   chopped

2 3/4 oz dates, chopped

1/3 cup candied cherries, chopped

2/3 cup raisins

1/2 cup milk

2 eggs, beaten

grated rind of 1 orange

5-6 tbsp orange juice

3 tbsp runny honey

1 Grease a 8 inch round cake pan and line the base with baking parchment.

2 Sift the flour, baking powder, and ground allspice into a large mixing bowl.

3 Rub in the butter with your fingers until the mixture resembles fine bread crumbs.

4 Carefully stir in the apricots, dates, candied cherries, and raisins with the milk, beaten eggs, grated orange rind and orange juice.

5 Stir in the honey and mix everything together to form a soft dropping consistency. Spoon into the prepared cake pan and level the surface.

6 Bake in a preheated oven, 350°F, for 1 hour until a fine skewer inserted into the center of the cake comes out clean.

7 Leave the cake to cool in the pan before turning out.

VARIATION

For a fruity alternative, replace the honey with 1 mashed ripe banana, if you prefer.

Eggless Sponge

*This is a healthy variation of the classic sponge layer cake
and is suitable for vegans.*

Makes one 8 inch cake

INGREDIENTS

1³/₄ cups self-rising whole-wheat
   flour
2 tsp baking powder

³/₄ cup superfine sugar
6 tbsp sunflower oil
1 cup water

1 tsp vanilla extract
4 tbsp strawberry or raspberry
   reduced-sugar spread
superfine sugar, for dusting

1   Grease two 8 inch sandwich layer pans and line them smoothly with baking parchment.

2   Sift the flour and baking powder into a large mixing bowl, stirring in any bran remaining in the sifter. Stir in the superfine sugar.

3   Pour in the sunflower oil, water, and vanilla extract and mix well with a wooden spoon for about 1 minute, or until the cake mixture reaches a smooth consistency.

4   Divide the mixture between the prepared pans.

5   Bake in a preheated oven, 350°F, for about 25-30 minutes until the center springs back when lightly touched. Leave to cool in the pans before turning out and transferring to a wire rack.

6   To serve, remove the baking parchment and place one of the sponges on to a serving plate. Spread with the jam and place the other sponge on top. Dust with a little superfine sugar.

VARIATION

Use melted vegan butter or margarine instead of the sunflower oil if you prefer, but allow it to cool before adding it to the dry ingredients in step 3.

Small Cakes & Cookies

This chapter contains everyday delights for chocolate fans. You are sure to be tempted by our wonderful array of cookies and small cakes. Make any day special with a home-made chocolate cookie to be served with coffee, as a snack or to accompany a special dessert. Although some take a little longer to make, most are quick and easy to prepare and decoration is often simple although you can get carried away if you like!

You'll find recipes for old favorites as well as some new cookies and small cakes to tickle your taste-buds. Finally, we have given the chocolate treatment to some traditional recipes, turning them into chocoholic delights, to tempt even the strongest-willed.

Meringues

These are just as meringues should be – as light as air and at the same time crisp and melt in the mouth.

Makes about 13

INGREDIENTS

4 egg whites
pinch of salt
¹/₂ cup granulated sugar

¹/₂ cup superfine sugar

1¹/₄ cups heavy cream, whipped lightly

1 Carefully line 3 baking sheets with sheets of baking parchment.

2 In a large clean bowl, whisk together the egg whites and salt until they are stiff, using an electric hand-held whisk or a balloon whisk. (You should be able to turn the bowl upside down without any movement from the egg whites.)

3 Whisk in the granulated sugar a little at a time; at this stage, the meringue should be starting to look glossy.

4 Sprinkle in the superfine sugar a little at a time and continue whisking until all the sugar has been incorporated and the meringue is thick, white and stands in tall peaks.

5 Transfer the meringue mixture to a pastry bag fitted with a ³/₄ inch star tip. Pipe about 26 small whirls on to the prepared baking sheets.

6 Bake in a preheated oven, 250°F, for 1¹/₂ hours or until the meringues are pale golden in color and can be easily lifted off

the paper. Leave them to cool in the turned-off oven overnight.

7 Just before serving, sandwich the meringues together in pairs with the cream and arrange on a serving plate.

VARIATION

For a finer texture, replace the granulated sugar with superfine sugar.

Rock Drops

These rock drops are more substantial than a crisp cookie.
Serve them fresh from the oven to enjoy them at their best.

Makes 8

INGREDIENTS

1³/4 cups all-purpose flour
2 tsp baking powder
¹/3 cup butter, cut into small pieces

¹/3 cup brown crystal sugar
¹/2 cup golden raisins

2 tbsp candied cherries, chopped
  finely
1 egg, beaten
2 tbsp milk

1 Lightly grease a baking sheet.

2 sift the flour and baking powder into a mixing bowl. Rub in the butter with your fingers until the mixture resembles bread crumbs.

3 Stir in the sugar, golden raisins and chopped candied cherries.

4 Add the beaten egg and the milk to the mixture and mix to form a soft dough.

5 Spoon 8 mounds of the mixture on to the baking sheet, spacing them well apart as they will spread while they are cooking.

6 Bake in a preheated oven, 400°F, for 15-20 minutes until firm to the touch when pressed with a finger.

7 Remove the rock drops from the baking sheet. Either serve very hot from the oven or transfer to a wire rack and leave to cool before serving.

COOK'S TIP

For convenience, prepare the dry ingredients in advance and just before cooking stir in the liquid.

Chocolate Biscotti

*These dry cookies are delicious served
with black coffee after a meal.*

Makes 16

INGREDIENTS

1 egg
$^{1}/_{3}$ cup superfine sugar
1 tsp vanilla extract

1 cup all-purpose flour
$^{1}/_{2}$ tsp baking powder
1 tsp ground cinnamon

1$^{3}/_{4}$ oz dark chocolate, chopped
roughly
1$^{3}/_{4}$ oz toasted slivered almonds
1$^{3}/_{4}$ oz pine nuts

1 Grease a large baking sheet.

2 Whisk the egg, sugar and vanilla extract in a mixing bowl with an electric mixer until it is thick and pale – ribbons of mixture should trail from the whisk as you lift it.

3 Sift the flour, baking powder, and cinnamon into a separate bowl, then sift into the egg mixture and fold in gently. Stir in the chocolate, almonds, and pine nuts.

4 Turn out on to a lightly floured surface and shape into a flat log about 9 inches long and $^{3}/_{4}$ inch wide. Transfer to the prepared baking sheet.

5 Bake in a preheated oven, 350°F, for 20-25 minutes or until golden. Remove from the oven and leave to cool for 5 minutes or until firm.

6 Transfer the log to a cutting board. Using a serrated bread knife, cut the log on the diagonal into slices about $^{1}/_{2}$ inch thick and

arrange them on the baking sheet. Cook for 10-15 minutes, turning halfway through the cooking time.

7 Leave to cool for about 5 minutes, then transfer to a wire rack to cool completely.

COOK'S TIP

*Store the biscotti in an
airtight container or jar and eat
within 2 weeks.*

Shortbread Fantails

*These cookies are perfect for afternoon tea or they can
be served with ice cream for a delicious dessert.*

Makes 8

INGREDIENTS

$^1/_2$ cup butter, softened
8 tsp granulated sugar
8 tsp confectioners' sugar
2 cups all-purpose flour

pinch of salt

2 tsp orange flower water
superfine sugar, for sprinkling

1 Lightly grease a 8 inch shallow round cake pan.

2 In a large mixing bowl, cream together the butter, the granulated sugar and the confectioners' sugar until light and fluffy.

3 Sift the flour and salt into the creamed mixture. Add the orange flower water and bring everything together to form a soft dough.

4 On a lightly floured surface, roll out the dough to a 8 inch round and place in the pan.

Prick the dough well and score into 8 triangles with a round-bladed knife.

5 Bake in a preheated oven, 300°F, for 30-35 minutes or until the cookie is pale golden and crisp.

6 Sprinkle with superfine sugar, then cut along the marked lines to make the fantails.

7 Leave the shortbread to cool before removing the pieces from the pan. Store in an airtight container.

COOK'S TIP

*For a crunchy addition, sprinkle
2 tablespoons of chopped mixed
nuts over the top of the fantails
before baking.*

Millionaire's Shortbread

*These rich squares of shortbread are topped with caramel and finished
with chocolate to make a very special treat!*

Makes 12 bars

INGREDIENTS

1¹/₂ cups all-purpose flour
¹/₂ cup butter, cut into small pieces

3 tbsp soft brown sugar, sifted

TOPPING:
10 tsp butter
3 tbsp soft brown sugar

14 oz can condensed milk
5¹/₂ oz milk chocolate

1 Grease a 9 inch square cake pan.

2 Sift the flour into a mixing bowl and rub in the butter with your fingers until the mixture resembles fine bread crumbs. Add the sugar and mix to form a firm dough.

3 Press the dough into the bottom of the prepared pan and prick with a fork.

4 Bake in a preheated oven, 375°F, for 20 minutes until

lightly golden. Leave to cool in the pan.

5 To make the topping, place the butter, sugar, and condensed milk in a non-stick saucepan and cook over a gentle heat, stirring constantly, until the mixture comes to a boil.

6 Reduce the heat and cook for 4-5 minutes until the caramel is pale golden and thick and is coming away from the sides of the pan. Pour the topping over the shortbread base and leave to cool.

7 When the caramel topping is firm, melt the milk chocolate in a heatproof bowl set over a saucepan of simmering water. Spread the melted chocolate over the topping, leave to set in a cool place, then cut the shortbread into squares or fingers to serve.

COOK'S TIP

Ensure the caramel layer is completely cool and set before coating it with the melted chocolate, otherwise they will mix together.

Lemon Jumbles

These lemony, melt-in-the-mouth cookies are made extra special by dredging with confectioners' sugar just before serving.

Makes about 50

INGREDIENTS

1/3 cup butter, softened	1 egg, beaten	1 tsp baking powder
1/2 cup superfine sugar	4 tbsp lemon juice	1 tbsp milk
grated rind of 1 lemon	3 cups all-purpose flour	confectioners' sugar, for dredging

1 Lightly grease several baking sheets.

2 In a mixing bowl, cream together the butter, superfine sugar, and lemon rind until pale and fluffy.

3 Add the beaten egg and lemon juice a little at a time, beating well after each addition.

4 Sift the flour and baking powder into the creamed mixture and blend together. Add the milk, mixing to form a dough.

5 Turn the dough out on to a lightly floured work surface and divide into about 50 equal-sized pieces.

6 Roll each piece into a sausage shape with your hands and twist in the middle to make an 'S' shape.

7 Place on the prepared cookie sheets and bake in a preheated oven, 325°F, for 15-20 minutes. Leave to cool completely on a wire rack. Dredge with confectioners' sugar to serve.

VARIATION

If you prefer, shape the dough into other shapes – letters of the alphabet or geometric shapes – or just make into round cookies.

Citrus Crescents

*For a sweet treat, try these cookies which
have a lovely citrus tang to them.*

Makes about 25

INGREDIENTS

$^1/_3$ cup butter, softened
$^1/_3$ cup superfine sugar
1 egg, separated

$1^3/_4$ cups all-purpose flour
grated rind of 1 orange
grated rind of 1 lemon

grated rind of 1 lime
2-3 tbsp orange juice
superfine sugar, for sprinkling
(optional)

1 Lightly grease 2 baking
sheets.

2 In a mixing bowl, cream
together the butter and sugar
until light and fluffy, then
gradually beat in the egg yolk.

3 Sift the flour into the
creamed mixture and mix
until evenly combined. Add the
orange, lemon, and lime rinds
to the mixture with enough of the
orange juice to make a soft dough.

4 Roll out the dough on a
lightly floured surface. Stamp
out rounds using a 3 inch cookie
cutter. Make crescent shapes by
cutting away a quarter of each
round. Re-roll the trimmings to
make about 25 crescents.

5 Place the crescents on to the
prepared baking sheets. Prick
the surface of each crescent with a
fork.

6 Lightly whisk the egg white
in a small bowl and brush it
over the cookies. Dust with extra
superfine sugar, if using.

7 Bake in a preheated oven,
400°F, for 12-15 minutes.
Leave the cookies to cool on a wire
rack before serving.

COOK'S TIP

*Store the citrus crescents in an
airtight container. Alternatively,
they can be frozen for up
to 1 month.*

Rosemary cookies

Do not be put off by the idea of herbs being used in these crisp cookies – try them and you will be pleasantly surprised.

Makes about 25

INGREDIENTS

10 tsp butter, softened
4 tbsp superfine sugar
grated rind of 1 lemon
4 tbsp lemon juice

1 egg, separated
2 tsp finely chopped fresh rosemary
1³/₄ cups all-purpose flour, sifted

superfine sugar, for sprinkling
(optional)

1 Lightly grease 2 baking sheets.

2 In a large mixing bowl, cream together the butter and sugar until pale and fluffy.

3 Add the lemon rind and juice, then the egg yolk and beat until they are thoroughly combined. Stir in the chopped fresh rosemary.

4 Add the sifted flour, mixing well until a soft dough is formed. Wrap and leave to chill for 30 minutes.

5 On a lightly floured surface, roll out the dough thinly and stamp out about 25 circles with a 2½ inch cookie cutter. Arrange the dough circles on the prepared baking sheets.

6 In a bowl, lightly whisk the egg white. Gently brush the egg white over the surface of each biscuit, then sprinkle with a little superfine sugar.

7 Bake in a preheated oven, 350°F, for about 15 minutes.

8 Transfer the cookies to a wire rack and leave to cool before serving.

COOK'S TIP

Store the cookies in an airtight container for up to 1 week.

VARIATION

In place of the fresh rosemary, use 1½ teaspoons of dried rosemary, if you prefer.

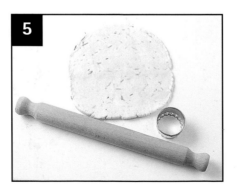

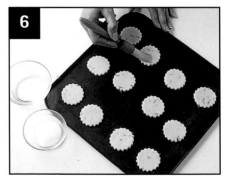

Oat & Raisin cookies

These oaty, fruity cookies
are delicious with a cup of tea!

Makes 10

INGREDIENTS

10 tsp butter
$^1/_2$ cup superfine sugar
1 egg, beaten

$^1/_2$ cup all-purpose flour
$^1/_2$ tsp salt
$^1/_2$ tsp baking powder

2 cups oatmeal
$^3/_4$ cup raisins
2 tbsp sesame seeds

1 Lightly grease 2 baking sheets.

2 In a large mixing bowl, cream together the butter and sugar until light and fluffy.

3 Add the beaten egg gradually and beat until well combined.

4 Sift the flour, salt, and baking powder into the creamed mixture. Mix well.

5 Add the porridge oats, raisins, and sesame seeds and mix together thoroughly.

6 Place spoonfuls of the mixture well apart on the prepared baking sheets and flatten them slightly with the back of a spoon.

7 Bake in a preheated oven, 350°F, for 15 minutes.

8 Leave the cookies to cool slightly on the baking sheets.

9 Transfer the cookies to a wire rack and leave to cool completely before serving.

COOK'S TIP

To enjoy these cookies at their best, store them in an airtight container.

VARIATION

Substitute chopped ready-to-eat dried apricots for the raisins, if you prefer.

Coconut Flapjacks

Freshly baked, these chewy flapjacks are just the thing for tea-time.

Makes 16 squares

INGREDIENTS

1 cup butter
1¹/₃ cups brown crystal sugar

2 tbsp light corn syrup
3¹/₂ cups oatmeal
1 cup shredded coconut

¹/₃ cup candied cherries, chopped

1 Lightly grease a 12 x 9 inch baking sheet.

2 Heat the butter, brown crystal sugar, and light corn syrup in a large saucepan until just melted.

3 Stir in the oats, shredded coconut and candied cherries and mix well until evenly combined.

4 Spread the mixture on to the baking sheet and press down with the back of a spatula to make a smooth surface.

5 Bake in a preheated oven, 325°F, for about 30 minutes.

6 Remove from the oven and leave to cool on the baking sheet for 10 minutes.

7 Cut the mixture into squares using a sharp knife.

8 Carefully transfer the flapjack squares to a wire rack and leave to cool completely.

COOK'S TIP

The flapjacks are best stored in an airtight container and eaten within 1 week. They can also be frozen for up to 1 month.

Hazelnut Squares

These can be made quickly and easily for an afternoon tea treat.
The chopped hazelnuts can be replaced by any other nut of your choice.

Makes 16

INGREDIENTS

$1^1/_4$ cups all-purpose flour
pinch of salt
1 tsp baking powder

$^1/_3$ cup butter, cut into small pieces
1 cup soft brown sugar
1 egg, beaten
4 tbsp milk

1 cup hazelnuts, halved
brown crystal sugar, for sprinkling
(optional)

1 Grease a 9 inch square cake pan and line the base with baking parchment.

2 Sift the flour, salt, and baking powder into a large mixing bowl.

3 Rub in the butter with your fingers until the mixture resembles fine bread crumbs. Stir in the brown sugar.

4 Add the egg, milk, and nuts to the mixture and stir well until thoroughly combined.

5 Spoon the mixture into the prepared cake pan and level the surface. Sprinkle with brown crystal sugar, if using.

6 Bake in a preheated oven, 350°F, for about 25 minutes or until the mixture is firm to the touch when pressed with a finger.

7 Leave to cool for 10 minutes, then loosen the edges with a round-bladed knife and turn out on to a wire rack. Cut into squares.

VARIATION

For a coffee time cookie, replace the milk with the same amount of cold strong black coffee, the stronger the better!

Gingernuts

Nothing compares to the taste of these freshly baked authentic gingernuts which have a lovely hint of orange flavor.

Makes 30

INGREDIENTS

3 cups self-rising flour
pinch of salt
1 cup superfine sugar

1 tbsp ground ginger
1 tsp baking soda
1/2 cup butter

1/4 cup light corn syrup
1 egg, beaten
1 tsp grated orange rind

1 Lightly grease several baking sheets.

2 Sift the flour, salt, sugar, ginger, and baking soda into a large mixing bowl.

3 Heat the butter and light corn syrup together in a saucepan over a very low heat until the butter has melted.

4 Leave the butter mixture to cool slightly, then pour it on to the dry ingredients.

5 Add the egg and orange rind and mix thoroughly.

6 Using your hands, carefully shape the dough into 30 even-sized balls.

7 Place the balls well apart on the prepared baking sheets, then flatten them slightly with your fingers.

8 Bake in a preheated oven, 325°F, for 15-20 minutes, then transfer them to a wire rack to cool.

COOK'S TIP

Store these biscuits in an airtight container and eat them within 1 week.

VARIATION

If you like your gingernuts crunchy, bake them in the oven for a few minutes longer.

Caraway cookies

The caraway seed is best known for its appearance in old-fashioned seed cake.
Here, caraway seeds give these cookies a very distinctive flavor.

Makes about 36

INGREDIENTS

2 cups all-purpose flour
pinch of salt
1/3 cup butter, cut into small pieces

1 1/4 cups superfine sugar
1 egg, beaten

2 tbsp caraway seeds
brown crystal sugar, for sprinkling
(optional)

1 Lightly grease several baking sheets.

2 Sift the flour and salt into a mixing bowl. Rub in the butter with your fingers until the mixture resembles fine bread crumbs. Stir in the superfine sugar.

3 Reserve 1 tablespoon of the beaten egg for brushing the cookies. Add the rest of the egg to the mixture along with the caraway seeds and bring together to form a soft dough.

4 On a lightly floured surface, roll out the cookie dough thinly and then cut out about 36 rounds with a 2½ inch cookie cutter.

5 Transfer the rounds to the prepared baking sheets, brush with the reserved egg and sprinkle with brown crystal sugar.

6 Bake in a preheated oven, 325°F, for 10-15 minutes until lightly golden and crisp.

7 Leave the cookies to cool on a wire rack and store in an airtight container.

VARIATION

Caraway seeds have a nutty, delicate anise flavor. If you don't like their flavor, replace the caraway seeds with the milder-flavored poppy seeds.

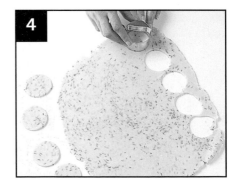

Peanut Butter Cookies

*These crunchy cookies will be popular with children
of all ages as they contain their favorite food – peanut butter.*

Makes 20

INGREDIENTS

$^1/_2$ cup butter, softened
$^1/_2$ cup chunky peanut butter
1 cup granulated sugar

1 egg, lightly beaten
1$^1/_4$ cup all-purpose flour
$^1/_2$ tsp baking powder

pinch of salt
2 $^3/_4$ oz unsalted peanuts, chopped

1 Lightly grease 2 baking
sheets.

2 In a large mixing bowl, beat
together the butter and
peanut butter.

3 Gradually add the granulated
sugar and beat well.

4 Add the beaten egg to the
mixture, a little at a time,
until it is thoroughly combined.

5 Sift the flour, baking powder,
and salt into the peanut
butter mixture.

6 Add the peanuts and bring all
of the ingredients together to
form a soft dough. Wrap and leave
to chill for about 30 minutes.

7 Form the dough into 20 balls
and place them on to the
prepared baking sheets about
2 inches apart to allow for
spreading. Flatten them slightly
with your hand.

8 Bake in a preheated oven,
375°F, for 15 minutes.
Transfer the cookies to a wire rack
and leave to cool

COOK'S TIP

*For a crunchy bite and sparkling
appearance, sprinkle the cookies
with brown crystal sugar before
baking.*

Spiced cookies

*These spicy cookies are perfect to serve with
fruit salad or ice cream for a very easy instant dessert.*

Makes about 24

INGREDIENTS

³/4 cup unsalted butter
1 cup dark muscovado sugar
2 cups all-purpose flour
pinch of salt
¹/2 tsp baking soda

1 tsp ground cinnamon
¹/2 tsp ground coriander
¹/2 tsp ground nutmeg
¹/4 tsp ground cloves
2 tbsp dark rum

1 Lightly grease 2 baking sheets.

2 Cream together the butter and sugar and whisk until light and fluffy.

3 Sift the flour, salt, baking soda, cinnamon, coriander, nutmeg, and cloves into the creamed mixture.

4 Stir the dark rum into the creamed mixture.

5 Using 2 teaspoons, place small mounds of the mixture, on to the baking sheets, placing them 3 inch apart to allow for spreading during cooking. Flatten each one slightly with the back of a spoon.

6 Bake in a preheated oven, 350°F, for 10-12 minutes until golden.

7 Leave the cookies to cool and crispen on wire racks before serving.

COOK'S TIP
*Use the back of a fork to flatten
the cookies slightly
before baking.*

Cinnamon & Sunflower Squares

These are moist cake-like squares with a lovely spicy flavor.

Makes 12

INGREDIENTS

1 cup butter, softened
1¼ cups superfine sugar
3 eggs, beaten

2 cups self-raising flour
½ tsp baking soda

1 tbsp ground cinnamon
⅔ cup sour cream
3½ oz sunflower seeds

1 Grease a 9 inch square cake pan and line the base with baking parchment.

2 In a large mixing bowl, cream together the butter and superfine sugar until the mixture is light and fluffy.

3 Gradually add the beaten eggs to the mixture, beating well after each addition.

4 Sift the self-raising flour, baking soda, and ground cinnamon into the creamed mixture and fold in gently, using a metal spoon.

5 Spoon in the sour cream and sunflower seeds and gently mix until well combined.

6 Spoon the mixture into the prepared cake pan and level the surface with the back of a spoon or a knife.

7 Bake in a preheated oven, 350°F, for about 45 minutes until the mixture is firm to the touch when pressed with a finger.

8 Loosen the edges with a round-bladed knife, then turn out on to a wire rack to cool completely. Slice into 12 squares.

COOK'S TIP

These moist squares will freeze well and will keep for up to 1 month.

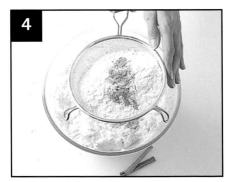

Apricot Slices

These vegan slices are ideal for packed lunches for children.
They are full of flavor and made with healthy ingredients.

Makes 12

INGREDIENTS

PASTRY:
1³/₄ cups whole-wheat flour
1³/₄ oz finely ground mixed nuts
¹/₃ cup vegan margarine, cut into
   small pieces
4 tbsp water
soya milk, to glaze

FILLING:
8 oz dried apricots
grated rind of 1 orange
1¹/₃ cups apple juice
1 tsp ground cinnamon
¹/₃ cup raisins

1 Lightly grease a 9 inch square cake pan. To make the pastry, place the flour and nuts in a mixing bowl and rub in the margarine with your fingers until the mixture resembles bread crumbs. Stir in the water and bring together to form a dough. Wrap and leave to chill for 30 minutes.

2 To make the filling, place the apricots, orange rind, and apple juice in a pan and bring to a boil. Simmer for 30 minutes until the apricots are mushy. Cool slightly, then blend to a paste. Stir in the cinnamon and raisins.

3 Divide the pastry in half, roll out one half and use to line the base of the pan. Spread the apricot paste over the top and brush the edges of the pastry with water. Roll out the rest of the dough to fit over the top of the apricot paste. Press down and seal the edges.

4 Prick the top of the pastry with a fork and brush with soya milk. Bake in a preheated oven, 400°F, for 20-25 minutes until the pastry is golden. Leave to cool slightly before cutting into 12 bars. Serve warm.

COOK'S TIP

These slices will keep in an airtight container for 3-4 days.

Cherry Biscuits

These are an alternative to traditional biscuits, using sweet candied cherries which not only create color but add a distinct flavor.

Makes 8

INGREDIENTS

2 cups self-rising flour
1 tbsp superfine sugar
pinch of salt

$^1/_3$ cup butter, cut into small pieces
3 tbsp candied cherries, chopped

3 tbsp golden raisins
1 egg, beaten
$^1/_4$ cup milk

1 Lightly grease a baking sheet.

2 sift the flour, sugar, and salt into a mixing bowl and rub in the butter with your fingers until the biscuit mixture resembles bread crumbs.

3 Stir in the candied cherries and golden raisins. Add the egg.

4 Reserve 1 tablespoon of the milk for glazing, then add the remainder to the mixture. Mix together to form a soft dough.

5 On a lightly floured surface, roll out the dough to a thickness of $^3/_4$ inches and cut out 8 biscuits, using a 2 inch cutter.

6 Place the biscuits on to the baking sheet and brush with the reserved milk.

7 Bake in a preheated oven, 425°F, for 8-10 minutes or until the biscuits are golden brown.

8 Leave to cool on a wire rack, then serve split and buttered.

COOK'S TIP

These biscuits will freeze very successfully but they are best defrosted and eaten within 1 month.

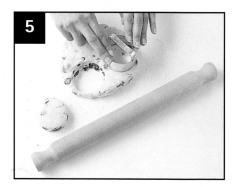

Molasses Biscuits

These biscuits are light and buttery like traditional biscuits, but they have a deliciously rich flavor which comes from the black molasses.

Makes 8

INGREDIENTS

2 cups self-rising flour
1 tbsp superfine sugar
pinch of salt

$\frac{1}{3}$ cup butter, cut into small pieces
1 eating apple, peeled, cored, and
  chopped

1 egg, beaten
2 tbsp black molasses
5 tbsp milk

1 Lightly grease a baking sheet.

2 Sift the flour, sugar, and salt into a mixing bowl.

3 Rub in the butter with your fingers until the mixture resembles fine bread crumbs.

4 Stir the chopped apple into the mixture until combined.

5 Mix the beaten egg, molasses, and milk together in a pitcher. Add to the dry ingredients to form a soft dough.

6 On a lightly floured working surface, roll out the dough to a thickness of $^3/_4$ inches and cut out 8 biscuits, using a 2 inch cutter.

7 Arrange the biscuits on the prepared baking sheet and bake in a preheated oven, 425°F, for 8-10 minutes.

8 Transfer the biscuits to a wire rack and leave to cool slightly.

9 Serve split in half and spread with butter.

COOK'S TIP

These biscuits can be frozen, but are best defrosted and eaten within 1 month.

Chocolate Orange cookies

These are delicious melt-in-the-mouth chocolate cookies with a tangy orange frosting.
Children love these cookies, especially if different shaped cutters are used.

Makes about 30

INGREDIENTS

¹/₃ cup butter, softened
¹/₃ cup superfine sugar
1 egg
1 tbsp milk
2 cups all-purpose flour

¹/₄ cup cocoa powder

FROSTING:
1 cup confectioners' sugar, sifted
3 tbsp orange juice
a little dark chocolate, melted

1 Carefully line 2 baking sheets with baking parchment.

2 Beat together the butter and sugar until light and fluffy. Beat in the egg and milk until well combined. Sift together the flour and cocoa powder and gradually mix together to form a soft dough. Use your fingers to incorporate the last of the flour and bring the dough together.

3 Roll out the dough on to a lightly floured surface until ¼ inch thick. Using a 2 inch fluted round cutter, cut out as many cookies as you can. Re-roll the dough trimmings and cut out more cookies.

4 Place the cookies on the prepared baking sheet and bake in a preheated oven, 350°F, for 10-12 minutes or until golden.

5 Leave the cookies to cool on the baking sheet for a few minutes, then transfer to a wire rack to cool completely.

6 To make the frosting, place the confectioners' sugar in a bowl and stir in enough orange juice to form a thin frosting that will coat the back of a spoon. Spread the frosting over the cookies and leave to set. Drizzle with melted chocolate. Leave the chocolate to set before serving.

Chocolate Crispy Bites

A favorite with children, this version of crispy bites have been given a new twist which is sure to be popular.

Makes 16

INGREDIENTS

WHITE LAYER:
4 tbsp butter
1 tbsp light corn syrup
5$^{1}/_{2}$ oz white chocolate

1$^{3}/_{4}$ oz toasted rice cereal

DARK LAYER:
4 tbsp butter
2 tbsp light corn syrup

dark chocolate, broken into small pieces
2$^{3}/_{4}$ oz toasted rice cereal

1 Grease a 8 inch square cake pan and line with baking parchment.

2 To make the white chocolate layer, melt the butter, light corn syrup and chocolate in a bowl set over a saucepan of gently simmering water.

3 Remove from the heat and stir in the rice cereal until it is well combined .

4 Press into the prepared pan and level the surface.

5 To make the dark chocolate layer, melt the butter, light corn syrup and dark chocolate in a bowl set over a pan of gently simmering water.

6 Remove from the heat and stir in the rice cereal until it is well coated. Pour the dark chocolate layer over the hardened white chocolate layer and chill until the top layer has hardened.

7 Turn out of the cake pan and cut into small squares, using a sharp knife.

COOK'S TIP

These bites can be made up to 4 days ahead. Keep them covered in the refrigerator until ready to use.

Chocolate Caramel Squares

Wonderfully rich, it is difficult to say 'No' to these cookies, which consist of a crunchy base, a creamy caramel filling and a chocolate top.

Makes 16

INGREDIENTS

generous ⅓ cup soft margarine
4 tbsp light muscovado sugar
1 cup all-purpose flour
½ cup rolled oats

CARAMEL FILLING:
2 tbsp butter
2 tbsp light muscovado sugar
7 oz can condensed milk

TOPPING:
3½ oz dark chocolate
1 oz white chocolate (optional)

1 Beat together the margarine and muscovado sugar in a bowl until light and fluffy. Beat in the flour and the rolled oats. Use your fingertips to bring the mixture together, if necessary.

2 Press the mixture into the base of a shallow 8 inch square cake pan.

3 Bake in a preheated oven, 350°F, for 25 minutes or until just golden and firm. Cool in the pan.

4 Place the ingredients for the caramel filling in a pan and heat gently, stirring until the sugar has dissolved and the ingredients combine. Bring slowly to a boil over a very low heat, then boil very gently for 3-4 minutes, stirring constantly until thickened.

5 Pour the caramel filling over the biscuit base in the pan and leave to set.

6 Melt the dark chocolate and spread it over the caramel. If using the white chocolate, melt it and pipe lines of white chocolate over the dark chocolate. Using a toothpick or a skewer, feather the white chocolate into the dark chocolate. Leave to set. Cut into squares to serve.

COOK'S TIP

If liked, you can line the pan with baking parchment so that the biscuit can be lifted out before cutting into pieces.

Chocolate Chip Brownies

Choose a good quality chocolate for these chocolate chip brownies to give them a rich flavor that is not too sweet.

Makes 12

INGREDIENTS

5$\frac{1}{2}$ oz dark chocolate, broken into pieces

1 cup butter, softened

2 cups self-rising flour

$\frac{1}{2}$ cup superfine sugar

4 eggs, beaten

2$\frac{3}{4}$ oz pistachio nuts, chopped

3$\frac{1}{2}$ oz white chocolate, chopped roughly

confectioners' sugar, for dusting

1 Lightly grease a 9 inch baking pan and line with waxed paper.

2 Melt the dark chocolate and butter in a heatproof bowl set over a saucepan of simmering water. Leave to cool slightly.

3 Sift the flour into a separate mixing bowl and stir in the superfine sugar.

4 Stir the eggs into the melted chocolate mixture, then pour this mixture into the flour and sugar mixture, beating well. Stir in the pistachio nuts and white chocolate, then pour the mixture into the pan, spreading it evenly into the corners.

5 Bake in a preheated oven, 350°, for 30-35 minutes until firm to the touch. Leave to cool in the pan for 20 minutes, then turn out on to a wire rack.

6 Dust the brownie with confectioners' sugar and cut into 12 pieces when cold.

COOK'S TIP

The brownie won't be completely firm in the middle when it is removed from the oven, but it will set when it has cooled.

Chocolate Chip Cookies

No chocolate cook's repertoire would be complete without a chocolate chip cookie recipe. This is sure to be a favorite as the basic recipe can be used to make several variations.

Makes about 18

INGREDIENTS

$1^{1}/_{2}$ cups all-purpose flour
1 tsp baking powder
$^{1}/_{2}$ cup soft margarine
$^{1}/_{2}$ cup light muscovado sugar

$^{1}/_{4}$ cup superfine sugar
$^{1}/_{2}$ tsp vanilla extract
1 egg
$^{2}/_{3}$ cup dark chocolate chips

1 Lightly grease 2 baking sheets.

2 Place all of the ingredients in a large mixing bowl and beat until well combined.

3 Place tablespoonfuls of the mixture on to the baking sheets, spacing them well apart to allow for spreading during cooking.

4 Bake in a preheated oven, 375°F, for 10-12 minutes or until the cookies are golden brown.

5 Using a spatula, transfer the cookies to a wire rack to cool completely.

VARIATIONS

For Choc & Nut Cookies, add $^{1}/_{2}$ cup chopped hazelnuts to the basic mixture.

For Double Choc Cookies, beat in $1^{1}/_{2}$ oz melted dark chocolate.

For White Chocolate Chip Cookies, use white chocolate chips instead of the dark chocolate chips.

VARIATIONS

For Mixed Chocolate Chip Cookies, use a mixture of dark, milk and white chocolate chips in the basic mixture.

For Chocolate Chip & Coconut Cookies, add $^{1}/_{3}$ cup shredded coconut to the basic mixture.

For Chocolate Chip & Raisin Cookies, add $1^{1}/_{2}$ oz/ 5 tbsp raisins to the basic mixture.

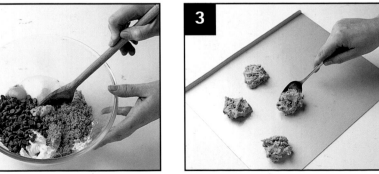

Chocolate Shortbread

*This buttery chocolate shortbread is the perfect addition
to the cookie tin of any chocoholic.*

Makes 12

INGREDIENTS

1¹/₂ cups all-purpose flour
1 tbsp cocoa powder
4 tbsp superfine sugar

²/₃ cup butter, softened
1³/₄ oz dark chocolate, chopped
finely

1 Lightly grease a baking sheet.

2 Place all of the ingredients in a large mixing bowl and beat together until they form a dough. Knead the dough lightly.

3 Place the dough on the prepared baking sheet and roll or press out to form a 8 inch circle.

4 Pinch the edges of the dough with your fingertips to form a decorative edge. Prick the dough all over with a fork and mark into 12 wedges, using a sharp knife.

5 Bake in a preheated oven, 325°F, for 40 minutes until firm and golden. Leave to cool slightly before cutting into wedges. Transfer to a wire rack to cool completely.

VARIATION

For round shortbread cookies, roll out the dough on a lightly floured surface to ¹/₃ inch thick. Cut out 3 inch rounds with a cookie cutter. Transfer to a greased baking sheet and bake as above. If liked, coat half the biscuit in melted chocolate.

VARIATION

The shortbread dough can be pressed into a floured shortbread mold and turned out on to the baking sheet before baking.

Chocolate Chip Flapjacks

Turn ordinary flapjacks into something special with the addition of some chocolate chips. Dark chocolate chips are used here, but you could use milk chocolate or white chocolate chips, if preferred.

Makes 12

INGREDIENTS

¹/₂ cup butter
¹/₃ cup superfine sugar
1 tbsp light corn syrup
4 cups rolled oats

¹/₂ cup dark chocolate chips
¹/₃ cup golden raisins

1 Lightly grease a shallow 8 inch square cake pan.

2 Place the butter, superfine sugar, and light corn syrup in a saucepan and cook over a low heat, stirring until the butter and sugar melt and the mixture is well combined.

3 Remove the pan from the heat and stir in the rolled oats until they are well coated. Add the chocolate chips and the golden raisins and mix well to combine everything.

4 Turn into the prepared pan and press down well.

5 Bake in a preheated oven, 350°F, for 30 minutes. Cool slightly, then mark into fingers. When almost cold cut into bars or squares and transfer to a wire rack until cold.

COOK'S TIP

The flapjacks will keep in an airtight container for up to 1 week, but they are so delicious they are unlikely to last that long!

VARIATION

For a really special flapjack, replace some of the oats with chopped nuts or sunflower seeds and a little extra dried fruit.

Chocolate Wheatmeals

*A good everyday cookie, these will keep well in an airtight container
for at least 1 week. Dip in white, milk or dark chocolate.*

Makes about 20

INGREDIENTS

$^1/_3$ cup butter

7 tbsp brown crystal sugar

1 egg

1 oz wheatgerm

1 cup whole-wheat self-rising flour

$^1/_2$ cup self rising flour, sifted

$4^1/_2$ oz chocolate

1 Lightly grease a baking sheet. Beat the butter and sugar until fluffy. Add the egg and beat well. Stir in the wheatgerm and flours. Bring the mixture together with your hands.

2 Roll rounded teaspoons of the mixture into balls and place on the prepared baking sheet, allowing room for the cookies to spread during cooking.

3 Flatten the cookies slightly with the prongs of a fork. Bake in a preheated oven, 350°F, for 15-20 minutes until golden.

Leave to cool on the sheet for a few minutes before transferring to a wire rack to cool completely.

4 Melt the chocolate, then dip each cookie in the chocolate to cover the bases and come a little way up the sides. Leave the excess to drip back into the bowl.

5 Place the cookies on a sheet of baking parchment and leave to set in a cool place before serving.

COOK'S TIP

These cookies can be frozen very successfully. Freeze them at the end of step 3 for up to 3 months. Defrost and then dip them in melted chocolate.

Malted Chocolate Wedges

These are perfect with a bedtime drink, although you can enjoy these tasty cookie wedges at any time of the day.

Makes 16

INGREDIENTS

generous ⅓ cup butter
2 tbsp light corn syrup
2 tbsp malted chocolate drink

8 oz malted milk cookies
2¾ oz milk or dark chocolate,
  broken into pieces
2 tbsp confectioners' sugar

2 tbsp milk

1 Grease a shallow 7 inch round cake pan or flan pan and line the base.

2 Place the butter, light corn syrup, and malted chocolate drink in a small pan and heat gently, stirring all the time until the butter has melted and the mixture is well combined.

3 Crush the cookies in a plastic bag with a rolling pin, or process them in a food processor until they form crumbs. Stir the crumbs into the chocolate mixture and mix well.

4 Press the mixture into the prepared pan and chill in the refrigerator until firm.

5 Place the chocolate pieces in a small heatproof bowl with the confectioners' sugar and the milk. Place the bowl over a pan of gently simmering water and stir until the chocolate melts and the mixture is combined.

6 Spread the chocolate frosting over the cookie base and leave to set in the pan. Using a sharp knife, cut into wedges to serve.

VARIATION

Add chopped pecan nuts to the cookie crumb mixture in step 3, if liked.

Chocolate & Coconut Squares

These cookies consist of a chewy coconut layer resting on a crisp chocolate biscuit base. Cut into squares to serve.

Makes 9

INGREDIENTS

8 oz dark chocolate graham crackers
$1/3$ cup butter or margarine
6 oz can evaporated milk
1 egg, beaten
1 tsp vanilla extract
5 tsp superfine sugar

$1/3$ cup self-rising flour, sifted
$1^1/3$ cups shredded coconut
$1^3/4$ oz dark chocolate (optional)

1 Grease a shallow 8 inch square cake pan and line the base.

2 Crush the crackers in a plastic bag with a rolling pin or process them in a food processor.

3 Melt the butter or margarine in a saucepan and stir in the crushed crackers until well combined.

4 Press the mixture into the base of the cake pan.

5 Beat together the evaporated milk, egg, vanilla, and sugar until smooth. Stir in the flour and shredded coconut. Pour over the biscuit base and level the top.

6 Bake in a preheated oven, 375°F, for 30 minutes or until the coconut topping is firm and just golden.

7 Leave to cool in the cake pan for about 5 minutes, then cut into squares. Leave to cool completely in the pan.

8 Carefully remove the squares from the pan and place them on a board. Melt the dark chocolate (if using) and drizzle it over the squares to decorate them. Leave the chocolate to set before serving.

COOK'S TIP

Store the squares in an airtight tin for up to 4 days. They can be frozen, undecorated, for up to 2 months. Defrost at room temperature.

No-Bake Chocolate Squares

These are handy little squares to keep in the refrigerator for when unexpected guest arrive.
Children will enjoy making these as an introduction to chocolate cookery.

Makes 16

INGREDIENTS

9$^1/_2$ oz dark chocolate
$^3/_4$ cup butter
4 tbsp light corn syrup
2 tbsp dark rum (optional)

6 oz plain cookies
1 oz toasted rice cereal
$^1/_2$ cup chopped walnuts or
  pecan nuts

$^1/_2$ cup candied cherries, chopped
  roughly
1 oz white chocolate, to decorate

1 Place the dark chocolate in a large mixing bowl with the butter, syrup, and rum, if using, and set over a saucepan of gently simmering water until melted, stirring until blended.

2 Break the cookies into small pieces and stir into the chocolate mixture along with the rice cereal, nuts, and cherries.

3 Line a 7inch square cake pan with baking parchment. Pour the mixture into the pan and level the top, pressing down well with the back of a spoon. Chill for 2 hours.

4 To decorate, melt the white chocolate and drizzle it over the top of the cake in a random pattern. Leave to set. To serve, carefully turn out of the pan and remove the baking parchment. Cut into 16 squares.

COOK'S TIP

Store in an airtight container in the refrigerator for up to 2 weeks.

VARIATION

Brandy or an orange-flavored liqueur can be used instead of the rum, if you prefer. Cherry brandy also works well.

VARIATION

For a coconut flavor, replace the rice cereal with shredded coconut and add a coconut-flavored liqueur.

Chocolate & Hazelnut Palmiers

These delicious chocolate and hazelnut cookies are very simple to make, yet so effective. For very young children, leave out the chopped nuts.

Makes about 26

INGREDIENTS

13 oz ready-made puff pastry
8 tbsp chocolate hazelnut spread

$1/2$ cup chopped toasted hazelnuts

5 tsp superfine sugar

1 Lightly grease a baking sheet. On a lightly floured surface, roll out the puff pastry to a rectangle about 15 × 9 inches in size.

2 Spread the chocolate hazelnut spread over the pastry using a spatula, then scatter the chopped hazelnuts over the top.

3 Roll up one long side of the pastry to the center, then roll up the other side so that they meet in the center. Where the pieces meet, dampen the edges with a little water to join them. Using a sharp knife, cut into thin slices.

Place each slice on to the prepared baking sheet and flatten slightly with a spatula. Sprinkle the slices with the superfine sugar.

4 Bake in a preheated oven, 425°F, for about 10-15 minutes until golden. Transfer to a wire rack to cool.

COOK'S TIP

Palmiers can be served cold, but they are also delicious served warm.

COOK'S TIP

The cookies can be frozen for up to 3 months in a rigid container.

VARIATION

For an extra chocolate flavor, dip the palmiers in melted dark chocolate to half-cover each biscuit.

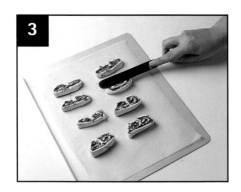

Sticky Chocolate Brownies

*Everyone loves chocolate brownies and these are so gooey
and delicious they are impossible to resist!*

Makes 9

INGREDIENTS

generous $^1/_3$ cup unsalted butter
$^3/_4$ cup superfine sugar
$^1/_2$ cup dark muscovado sugar
$4^1/_2$ oz dark chocolate
1 tbsp light corn syrup
2 eggs

1 tsp chocolate or vanilla extract
$^3/_4$ cup all-purpose flour
2 tbsp cocoa powder
$^1/_2$ tsp baking powder

1 Lightly grease a 8 inch shallow square cake pan and line the base.

2 Place the butter, sugars, dark chocolate, and light corn syrup in a heavy-bottomed saucepan and heat gently, stirring until the mixture is well blended and smooth. Remove from the heat and leave to cool.

3 Beat together the eggs and extract. Whisk in the cooled chocolate mixture.

4 Sift together the flour, cocoa powder, and baking powder and fold carefully into the egg and chocolate mixture, using a metal spoon or a spatula.

5 Spoon the mixture into the prepared pan and bake in a preheated oven, 350°F, for 25 minutes until the top is crisp and the edge of the cake is beginning to shrink away from the pan. The inside of the cake mixture will still be quite stodgy and soft to the touch.

6 Leave the cake to cool completely in the pan, then cut it into squares to serve.

COOK'S TIP

This cake can be well wrapped and frozen for up to 2 months. Defrost at room temperature for about 2 hours or overnight in the refrigerator.

Chocolate Fudge Brownies

Chocolate brownies are very popular, here a traditional brownie mixture has a cream cheese ribbon through the center and is topped with a delicious chocolate fudge frosting.

Makes 16

INGREDIENTS

7 oz low-fat soft cheese
$^1/_2$ tsp vanilla extract
2 eggs
generous 1 cup superfine sugar
generous $^1/_3$ cup butter
3 tbsp cocoa powder
$^3/_4$ cup self-rising flour, sifted

$1^3/_4$ oz pecans, chopped

FUDGE FROSTING:
1 tbsp butter
1 tbsp milk
$^1/_2$ cup confectioners' sugar
2 tbsp cocoa powder
pecans, to decorate (optional)

1 Lightly grease a 8 inch square shallow cake pan and line the base.

2 Beat together the cheese, vanilla extract and 5 tsp of the superfine sugar until smooth, then set aside.

3 Beat the eggs and remaining superfine sugar together until light and fluffy. Place the butter and cocoa powder in a small pan and heat gently, stirring until the butter melts and the mixture combines, then stir it into the egg mixture. Fold in the flour and nuts.

4 Pour half of the brownie mixture into the pan and level the top. Carefully spread the soft cheese over it, then cover it with the remaining brownie mixture. Bake in a preheated oven, 350°F, for 40-45 minutes. Cool in the pan.

5 To make the frosting, melt the butter in the milk. Stir in the confectioners' sugar and cocoa powder. Spread the frosting over the brownies and decorate with pecan nuts, if using. Leave the frosting to set, then cut into squares to serve.

VARIATION

Omit the cheese layer if preferred.
Use walnuts in place of the pecans.

Chocolate Chip Muffins

Muffins are always popular and are so simple to make. I make mini muffins for my young children which are fabulous bite-size treats or perfect for children parties.

Makes 12

INGREDIENTS

generous ¹/₃ cup soft margarine

1 cup superfine sugar

2 large eggs

²/₃ cup whole milk unsweetened
   yogurt

5 tbsp milk

2 cups all-purpose flour

1 tsp baking soda

6 oz dark chocolate chips

1 Line 12 muffin pans with paper cases.

2 Place the margarine and sugar in a large mixing bowl and beat with a wooden spoon until light and fluffy. Beat in the eggs, yogurt and milk until combined.

3 Sift the flour and baking soda together and add to the mixture. Stir until just blended.

4 Stir in the chocolate chips, then spoon the mixture into the paper cases and bake in a preheated oven, 375°F, for 25 minutes or until a fine skewer inserted into the center comes out clean. Leave to cool in the pan for 5 minutes, then turn out on to a wire rack to cool completely.

VARIATION

The mixture can also be used to make 6 large or 24 mini muffins. Bake mini muffins for 10 minutes or until springy to the touch.

VARIATION

For chocolate and orange muffins, add the grated rind of 1 orange and replace the milk with fresh orange juice.

Chocolate Cookies

A plain cookie mixture is transformed into a chocoholics treat
by the simple addition of chocolate chips.

Makes 9

INGREDIENTS

2 cups self-rising flour, sifted
1/4 cup butter

1 tbsp superfine sugar
1/3 cup chocolate chips

about 2/3 cup milk

1 Lightly grease a baking sheet. Place the flour in a mixing bowl. Cut the butter into small pieces and rub it into the flour with your fingertips; do this until the biscuit mixture resembles fine bread crumbs.

2 Stir in the superfine sugar and chocolate chips.

3 Mix in enough milk to form a soft dough.

4 On a lightly floured surface, roll out the dough to form a rectangle 4 × 6 inches, about 1 inch thick. Cut the dough into 9 squares.

5 Place the cookies spaced well apart on the prepared baking sheet.

6 Brush with a little milk and bake in a preheated oven, 425°F, for 10-12 minutes until the cookies are risen and golden.

COOK'S TIP

To be at their best, all cookies
should be freshly baked and served
warm. Split the warm cookies and
spread them with a little chocolate
and hazelnut spread or a good
dollop of whipped cream.

VARIATION

Use dark, milk or white chocolate
chips or a mixture of all three. Use
a 2 inch cookie cutter to cut out
round cookies, if preferred.

Choc-Chip Tartlets

These tasty little tartlets will be a big hit with the kids.
Serve as a dessert or a special teatime treat.

Makes 6

INGREDIENTS

1³/₄ oz toasted hazelnuts
1³/₄ cups all-purpose flour
1 tbsp confectioners' sugar
¹/₃ cup soft margarine

FILLING:
2 tbsp cornstarch
1 tbsp cocoa powder
1 tbsp superfine sugar
1¹/₄ cups semi-skimmed milk
3 tbsp chocolate and hazelnut spread
2¹/₂ tbsp dark chocolate chips

2¹/₂ tbsp milk chocolate chips
2¹/₂ tbsp white chocolate chips

1 Finely chop the nuts in a food processor. Add the flour, the 1 tbsp sugar, and the margarine. Process for a few seconds until the mixture resembles bread crumbs. Add 2-3 tbsp water and process to form a soft dough. Cover and chill in the freezer for 10 minutes.

2 Roll out the dough and use it to line six 4 inch loose-bottomed tartlet pans. Prick the bases with a fork and line them with loosely crumpled foil. Bake in a preheated oven, 400°F, for 15 minutes. Remove the foil and bake for a further 5 minutes until the pie shells are crisp and golden. Remove from the oven and leave to cool.

3 Mix together the cornstarch, cocoa powder, and sugar with enough milk to make a smooth paste. Stir in the remaining milk. Pour into a pan and cook gently over a low heat, stirring until thickened. Stir in the hazelnut and chocolate spread.

4 Mix together the chocolate chips and reserve a quarter. Stir half of the remaining chips into the custard. Cover with damp waxed paper and leave until almost cold, then stir in the second half of the chocolate chips. Spoon the mixture into the pie shells and leave to cool. Decorate with the reserved chips, scattering them over the top.

Chocolate Cup Cakes with White Chocolate Frosting

A variation on an old favorite, both kids and grown-ups
will love these sumptuous little cakes.

Makes 18

INGREDIENTS

generous $^1/_3$ cup butter, softened
7 tbsp superfine sugar
2 eggs, lightly beaten
$^1/_3$ cup dark chocolate chips
2 tbsp milk

$1^1/_4$ cups self-rising flour
$^1/_4$ cup cocoa powder

FROSTING:
8 oz white chocolate
$5^1/_2$ oz low-fat soft cheese

1 Line an 18 hole bun tray with individual paper shells.

2 Beat together the butter and sugar until pale and fluffy. Gradually add the eggs, beating well after each addition. Add a little of the flour if the mixture begins to curdle. Add the milk, then fold in the chocolate chips.

3 Sift together the flour and cocoa powder and fold into the mixture with a metal spoon or spatula. Divide the mixture equally between the paper shells and level the tops.

4 Bake in a preheated oven, 350°F, for 20 minutes, or until well risen and springy to the touch. Leave to cool on a wire rack.

5 To make the frosting, melt the chocolate, then leave to cool slightly. Beat the cream cheese until softened slightly, then beat in the melted chocolate. Spread a little of the frosting over each cake and chill for 1 hour before serving.

VARIATION

Add white chocolate chips or chopped pecan nuts to the mixture instead of the dark chocolate chips, if you prefer. You can also add the finely grated rind of 1 orange for a chocolate and orange flavor.

Chocolate Butterfly Cakes

*Filled with a tangy lemon cream these appealing cakes
will be a favorite with adults and children alike.*

Makes 12

INGREDIENTS

¹/₂ cup soft margarine
¹/₂ cup superfine sugar
1¹/₄ cups self-rising flour
2 large eggs
2 tbsp cocoa powder
1 oz dark chocolate,
  melted

LEMON BUTTER CREAM:
generous ¹/₃ cup unsalted butter,
  softened
1¹/₃ cups confectioners' sugar, sifted
grated rind of ¹/₂ lemon
1 tbsp lemon juice
confectioners' sugar, to dust

1 Place 12 paper shells in a bun tray. Place all of the ingredients for the cakes, except for the melted chocolate, in a large mixing bowl and beat with electric beaters until the mixture is just smooth. Beat in the chocolate.

2 Spoon equal amounts of the cake mixture into each paper shell, filling them three-quarters full. Bake in a preheated oven, 350°F, for 15 minutes or until springy to the touch. Transfer the cakes to a wire rack and leave to cool.

3 To make the lemon butter cream, place the butter in a mixing bowl and beat until fluffy, then gradually beat in the confectioners' sugar. Beat in the lemon rind and gradually add the lemon juice, beating well.

4 When cold, cut the top off each cake, using a serrated knife. Cut each top in half.

5 Spread or pipe the butter cream frosting over the cut surface of each cake and push the 2 cut pieces of cake top into the frosting to form wings. Sprinkle with confectioners' sugar.

VARIATION

For a chocolate butter cream, beat the butter and confectioners' sugar together, then beat in 1 oz melted dark chocolate.

Puddings & Desserts

Chocolate is comforting at anytime but no more so than when served in a steaming hot pudding. It is hard to think of anything more warming, comforting, and homely than tucking into a steamed hot Chocolate Fudge Pudding or a Chocolate Charlotte. The child in us will love the chocolate addition to nursery favorites such as Bread & Butter Pudding. In fact, there are several old favorites that have been given the chocolate treatment, bringing them bang up to date and putting them on the chocolate lovers map.

When you are feeling in need of something a little more sophisticated, try the new-style Chocolate Apple Pancake Stack, or Chocolate Pear & Almond Flan, which might be more in keeping. Or try Chocolate Zabaglione for a sophisticated creamy, warm dessert set to get your taste buds in a whirl!

This chapter is packed full of chocolate delights, with different tastes and textures to add warmth to any day.

Fruit Crumble

Any fruits in season can be used in this wholesome pudding.
It is suitable for vegans as it contains no dairy produce.

Serves 6

INGREDIENTS

6 eating pears, peeled, cored,
　quartered and sliced
1 tbsp candied ginger, chopped
1 tbsp dark muscovado sugar
2 tbsp orange juice
TOPPING:
1¹/₂ cups all-purpose flour

¹/₃ cup vegan margarine, cut into
　small pieces
1 oz almonds, slivered
¹/₃ cup oatmeal
50 g/1³/₄ oz dark muscovado sugar
soya custard, to serve

1 Lightly grease a 4¹/₂ cup ovenproof dish.

2 In a bowl, mix together the pears, ginger, dark muscovado sugar, and orange juice. Spoon the mixture into the prepared dish.

3 To make the crumble topping, sift the flour into a mixing bowl and rub in the margarine with your fingers until the mixture resembles fine breadcrumbs. Stir in the slivered almonds, porridge oats, and dark muscovado sugar. Mix until well combined.

4 Sprinkle the crumble topping evenly over the pear and ginger mixture in the dish.

5 Bake in a preheated oven, 375°F, for 30 minutes until the topping is golden and the fruit tender. Serve with soya custard, if using.

VARIATION

Stir 1 tsp ground allspice into the crumble mixture in step 3 for added flavor, if you prefer.

Pineapple Upside-Down Cake

This upside-down cake shows how a classic favorite can be adapted for vegans by making the cake with vegan margarine and oil instead of butter and eggs.

Serves 6

INGREDIENTS

15 oz can unsweetened pineapple
pieces, drained and juice reserved
4 tsp cornstarch
3 tbsp soft brown sugar
10 tsp vegan margarine, cut into
small pieces
$1/2$ cup water

rind of 1 lemon

SPONGE:
$1/4$ cup sunflower oil
$1/3$ cup soft brown sugar
$2/3$ cup water
$1^1/4$ cups all-purpose flour

2 tsp baking powder
1 tsp ground cinnamon

1 Grease a deep 7 inch cake pan. Mix the reserved juice from the pineapple with the cornstarch until it forms a smooth paste. Put the paste in a saucepan with the sugar, margarine, and water and stir over a low heat until the sugar has dissolved. Bring to a boil and simmer for 2-3 minutes until thickened. Leave to cool slightly.

2 To make the sponge, place the oil, sugar, and water in a saucepan. Heat gently until the sugar has dissolved; do not allow it to boil. Remove from the heat and leave to cool. sift the flour, baking powder, and ground cinnamon into a mixing bowl. Pour over the cooled sugar syrup and beat well to form a batter.

3 Place the pineapple pieces and lemon rind on the bottom of the pan and pour over 4 tablespoons of the pineapple syrup. Spoon the sponge batter on top.

4 Bake in a preheated oven, 350°F, for 35-40 minutes until set and a fine metal skewer inserted into the center comes out clean. Invert on to a plate, leave to stand for 5 minutes, then remove the pan. Serve with the remaining syrup.

VARIATION

Add 1 oz golden raisins to the pineapple pieces, if you prefer.

Mincemeat & Grape Jalousie

This jalousie makes a good Christmas-time dessert. Its festive
filling and flavor is a great alternative to mince pies.

Serves 4

INGREDIENTS

1lb fresh ready-made puff pastry	3$\frac{1}{2}$ oz grapes, seeded and halved	brown crystal sugar,
14$\frac{1}{2}$ oz jar mincemeat	1 egg, for glazing	for sprinkling

1 Lightly grease a baking sheet.

2 On a lightly floured surface, roll out the pastry and cut it into 2 oblongs.

3 Place one pastry oblong on to the prepared baking sheet and brush the edges with water.

4 Combine the mincemeat and grapes in a mixing bowl. Spread the mixture over the pastry oblong on the baking sheet, leaving a 1 inch border.

5 Fold the second pastry oblong in half lengthways, and carefully cut a series of parallel lines across the folded edge, leaving a 1 inch border.

6 Open out the pastry oblong and lay it over the mincemeat. Seal down the edges of the and press together well.

7 Flute and crimp the edges of the pastry. Lightly brush with the beaten egg and sprinkle with brown crystal sugar.

8 Bake in a preheated oven, 425°F, for 15 minutes. Lower the heat to 350°F and cook for a further 30 minutes until the jalousie is well risen and golden brown. Leave to cool on a wire rack before serving.

COOK'S TIP

For an enhanced festive flavor, stir 2 tbsp sherry into the mincemeat.

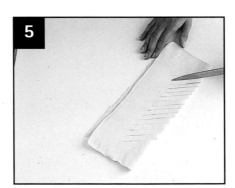

Apricot & Cranberry Frangipane Tart

This tart is ideal to make at Christmas time when fresh cranberries are in abundance.
If liked, brush the warm tart with 2 tbsp melted apricot jam.

Serves 8-10

INGREDIENTS

PASTRY:
$1/4$ cups all-purpose flour
$1/2$ cup superfine sugar
$1/2$ cup butter, cut into small pieces
1 tbsp water
FILLING:
1 cup unsalted butter
1 cup superfine sugar

1 egg
2 egg yolks
6 tbsp all-purpose flour, sifted
$1^2/3$ cups ground almonds
4 tbsp heavy cream
$14^1/2$ oz can apricot halves, drained
$4^1/2$ oz fresh cranberries

1 To make the pastry, place the flour and sugar in a bowl and rub in the butter with your fingers. Add the water and work the mixture together until a soft pastry has formed. Wrap and leave to chill for 30 minutes.

2 On a lightly floured surface, roll out the dough and line a $9^1/2$ inch loose-bottomed flan pan. Prick the pastry with a fork and leave to chill for 30 minutes.

3 Line the pie shell with foil and baking beans and bake in a preheated oven, 375°F, for 15 minutes. Remove the foil and baking beans and cook for a further 10 minutes.

4 To make the filling, cream together the butter and sugar until light and fluffy. Beat in the egg and egg yolks, then stir in the flour, almonds, and cream.

5 Place the apricot halves and cranberries on the bottom of the pie shell and spoon the filling over the top.

6 Bake in the oven for about 1 hour, or until the topping is just set. Leave to cool slightly, then serve warm or cold.

Orange Tart

*This is a variation of the classic lemon tart – in this recipe
fresh bread crumbs are used to create a thicker texture.*

Serves 6-8

INGREDIENTS

PASTRY:
1¼ cups all-purpose flour
5 tsp superfine sugar
½ cup butter, cut into small pieces
1 tbsp water

FILLING:
grated rind of 2 oranges
9 tbsp orange juice
1 cup fresh white bread crumbs
2 tbsp lemon juice

⅔ cup light cream
¼ cup butter
¼ cup superfine sugar
2 eggs, separated
pinch of salt

1 To make the pastry, place the flour and sugar in a bowl and rub in the butter with your fingers. Add the cold water and work the mixture together until a soft pastry has formed. Wrap and leave to chill for 30 minutes.

2 Roll out the dough and line a 9½ inch loose-bottomed flan pan. Prick the pastry with a fork and leave to chill for 30 minutes.

3 Line the pie shell with foil and baking beans and bake in a preheated oven, 375°F, for 15 minutes. Remove the foil and beans and cook for 15 minutes.

4 To make the filling, mix the orange rind and juice and the bread crumbs in a bowl. Stir in the lemon juice and light cream. Melt the butter and sugar in a pan over a low heat. Remove the pan from the heat, add the 2 egg yolks, the salt, and the bread crumb mixture and stir.

5 In a mixing bowl, whisk the egg whites with a pinch of salt until they form soft peaks. Fold them into the egg yolk mixture.

6 Pour the filling mixture into the pie shell. Bake in a preheated oven, 325°F, for about 45 minutes or until just set. Leave to cool slightly and serve warm.

Lemon Tart

*No-one will be able to resist this tart with its buttery pastry
and a sharp, melt-in-the-mouth lemon filling.*

Serves 8

INGREDIENTS

PASTRY:
1¼ cups all-purpose flour
5 tsp superfine sugar
½ cup butter, cut into small pieces
1 tbsp water

FILLING:
⅔ cup heavy cream
½ cup superfine sugar
4 eggs
grated rind of 3 lemons
12 tbsp lemon juice

confectioners' sugar,
for dusting

1 To make the pastry, place the flour and sugar in a bowl and rub in the butter using your fingers. Add the water and mix until a soft pastry has formed. Wrap and leave to chill for 30 minutes.

2 On a lightly floured surface, roll out the dough and line a 9½ inch loose-bottomed flan pan. Prick the pastry with a fork and leave to chill for 30 minutes.

3 Line the pie shell with foil and baking beans and bake in a preheated oven, 375°F, for 15 minutes. Remove the foil and baking beans and cook for a further 15 minutes.

4 To make the filling, whisk the cream, sugar, eggs, lemon rind, and juice together. Place the pie shell, still in its pan, on a baking sheet and pour in the filling.

5 Bake in the oven for about 20 minutes or until just set. Leave to cool, then lightly dust with confectioners' sugar before serving.

COOK'S TIP

To avoid any spillage, pour half of the filling into the pie shell, place in the oven and pour in the remaining filling.

Apple & Mincemeat Tart

*The fresh apple brings out the flavor of the sweet rich mincemeat
and makes it a beautifully moist filling for pies and tarts.*

Serves 8

INGREDIENTS

PASTRY:
1¼ cups all-purpose flour
5 tsp superfine sugar
½ cup butter, cut
  into small pieces
1 tbsp water

FILLING:
14½ oz jar mincemeat
3 eating apples, cored and grated
1 tbsp lemon juice
6 tsp light corn syrup
9 tsp butter

1 To make the pastry, place the flour and superfine sugar in a large mixing bowl and rub in the butter with your fingertips.

2 Add the water and work the mixture together until a soft pastry has formed. Wrap and leave to chill in the refrigerator for 30 minutes.

3 On a lightly floured surface, roll out the dough and line a 9½ inch loose-bottomed flan pan. Prick the dough with a fork and leave to chill for 30 minutes.

4 Line the pie shell with foil and baking beans. Bake the shell in a preheated oven, 375°F, for 15 minutes. Remove the foil and beans and cook for 15 minutes.

5 Combine the mincemeat with the apples and lemon juice and spoon into the baked pie shell.

6 Melt the syrup and butter together and pour it over the mincemeat mixture.

7 Return the tart to the oven and bake for about 20 minutes or until firm. Serve warm.

VARIATION

Add 2 tbsp sherry to spice up the mincemeat, if you wish.

Pine Nut Tart

This tart has a sweet filling made with creamy cheese and it is topped with pine nuts for a decorative finish.

Serves 8

INGREDIENTS

PASTRY:
1/4 cups all-purpose flour
5 tsp superfine sugar
1/2 cup butter, cut into small pieces
1 tbsp water

FILLING:
12 oz curd cheese

4 tbsp heavy cream
3 eggs
1/2 cup superfine sugar
grated rind of 1 orange
3 1/2 oz pine nuts

1 To make the pastry, place the flour and sugar in a bowl and rub in the butter with your fingers. Add the water and work the mixture together until a soft pastry has formed. Wrap and leave to chill for 30 minutes.

2 On a lightly floured surface, roll out the dough and line a 9½ inch loose-bottomed flan pan. Prick the pastry with a fork and leave to chill for 30 minutes.

3 Line the pie shell with foil and baking beans and bake in a preheated oven, 375°F, for 15 minutes. Remove the foil and beans and cook the pie shell for a further 15 minutes.

4 To make the filling, beat together the curd cheese, cream, eggs, sugar, orange rind, and half of the pine nuts. Pour the filling into the pie shell and sprinkle over the remaining pine nuts.

5 Bake in the oven at 325°F for 35 minutes or until just set. Leave to cool before serving.

VARIATION

Replace the pine nuts with slivered almonds, if you prefer.

Crème Brûlée Tarts

Serve these tarts with fresh fruit, if wished.

Makes 6

INGREDIENTS

PASTRY:
1¼ cups all-purpose flour
5 tsp superfine sugar
½ cup butter, cut into small pieces
1 tbsp water

FILLING:
4 egg yolks
1¾ oz superfine sugar

1¾ cups heavy cream
1 tsp vanilla extract
brown crystal sugar,
   for sprinkling

1 To make the pastry, place the flour and sugar in a bowl and rub in the butter with your fingers. Add the water and work the mixture together until a soft pastry has formed. Wrap and leave to chill for 30 minutes.

2 On a lightly floured surface, roll out the dough to line six 4 inch tart pans. Prick the bottom of the pastry with a fork and leave to chill for 20 minutes.

3 Line the pie shells with foil and baking beans and bake in a preheated oven, 375°F, for 15 minutes. Remove the foil and beans and cook for 10 minutes until crisp and golden. Leave to cool.

4 Meanwhile, make the filling. In a bowl, beat the egg yolks and sugar until pale. Heat the cream and vanilla extract in a pan until just below boiling point, then pour it onto the egg mixture, whisking constantly.

5 Return the mixture to a clean pan and bring to just below a boil, stirring, until thick. Do not allow to boil or it will curdle.

6 Leave the mixture to cool slightly, then pour it into the tart pans. Leave to cool and then leave to chill overnight.

7 Sprinkle the tarts with the sugar. Place under a preheated hot broiler for a few minutes. Leave to cool, then chill for 2 hours before serving.

Pear Tarts

These tarts are made with ready-made puff pastry which is available from most supermarkets. The finished pastry is rich and buttery.

Serves 6

INGREDIENTS

9 oz fresh ready-made
  puff pastry
1 oz soft brown sugar

1 oz butter (plus extra for brushing)
1 tbsp candied ginger, finely chopped

3 pears, peeled, halved, and cored
cream, to serve

1 On a lightly floured surface, roll out the pastry. Cut out six 4 inch round circles.

2 Place the circles on to a large baking sheet and leave to chill for 30 minutes.

3 Cream together the brown sugar and butter in a small bowl, then stir in the chopped candied ginger.

4 Prick the pastry circles with a fork and spread a little of the ginger mixture on to each one.

5 Slice the pear halves lengthways – but keeping them intact at the tip. Fan out the slices slightly.

6 Place a fanned-out pear half on top of each pastry circle. Make small flutes around the edge of the pastry circles and brush each pear half with melted butter.

7 Bake in a preheated oven, 400°F, for 15-20 minutes until the pastry is well risen and golden. Serve warm with a little cream.

COOK'S TIP

If you prefer, serve these tarts with vanilla ice cream for a delicious dessert.

Cheese & Apple Tart

The chopped apples and dates and the soft brown sugar in the filling make this a sweet tart with a savory twist to it!

Serves 8

INGREDIENTS

1¹/₂ cups self-rising flour
1 tsp baking powder
pinch of salt
¹/₃ cup soft brown sugar

3¹/₂ oz pitted dates, chopped
1lb eating apples, cored and chopped
¹/₄ cup walnuts, chopped

¹/₄ cup sunflower oil
2 eggs
6 oz Red Leicester cheese, grated

1 Grease a 9½ inch loose-bottomed flan pan and line it smoothly with baking parchment.

2 Sift the flour, baking powder, and salt into a bowl. Stir in the brown sugar and the chopped dates, apples, and walnuts. Mix them together until well combined.

3 Beat the oil and eggs together and add them to the mixture of dry ingredients. Stir until they are well combined.

4 Spoon half of the mixture into the pan and level the surface with the back of a spoon.

5 Sprinkle with the cheese, then spoon over the remaining cake mix, spreading it to the edges of the pan.

6 Bake in a preheated oven, 350°F, for 45-50 minutes or until golden and firm to the touch.

7 Leave to cool slightly in the tin. Serve warm.

COOK'S TIP

This is a deliciously moist tart. Any leftovers should be stored in the refrigerator and heated to serve.

Pavlova

This delicious dessert originated in Australia. Serve it with
sharp fruits to balance the sweetness of the meringue.

Serves 6

INGREDIENTS

3 egg whites
pinch of salt
3/4 cup superfine sugar

1 1/4 cups heavy cream, lightly
whipped

fresh fruit of your choice (raspberries,
strawberries, peaches, passion fruit,
cape gooseberries)

1 Carefully line a baking sheet with a sheet of baking parchment.

2 Whisk the egg whites with the salt in a large bowl until they form soft peaks.

3 Whisk in the sugar a little at a time, whisking well after each addition until all of the sugar has been incorporated.

4 Spoon three-quarters of the meringue on to the baking sheet, forming a round 8 inches in diameter.

5 Place spoonfuls of the remaining meringue all around the edge of the round so they join up to make a nest shape.

6 Bake in a preheated oven, 275°F, for 1 1/4 hours.

7 Turn the heat off, but leave the pavlova in the oven until it is completely cold.

8 To serve, place the pavlova on a serving dish. Spread with the lightly whipped cream, then arrange the fresh fruit on top.

COOK'S TIP

It is a good idea to make the pavlova in the evening and leave it in the turned-off oven overnight.

VARIATION

If you are worried about making the round shape, draw a circle on the baking parchment, turn the paper over, then spoon the meringue inside the shape.

Raspberry Shortcake

For this lovely summery dessert, two crisp rounds of shortbread are sandwiched together with fresh raspberries and lightly whipped cream.

Serves 8

INGREDIENTS

1½ cups self-rising flour
⅓ cup butter, cut into cubes
⅓ cup superfine sugar
1 egg yolk
1 tbsp rose water

2½ cups whipping cream, whipped lightly
8 oz raspberries, plus a few for decoration

TO DECORATE:
confectioners' sugar
mint leaves

1 Lightly grease 2 cookie sheets.

2 To make the shortcakes, sift the flour into a bowl.

3 Rub the butter into the flour with your fingers until the mixture resembles bread crumbs.

4 Stir the sugar, egg yolk, and rose water into the mixture and bring together with your fingers to form a soft dough. Divide the dough in half.

5 Roll each piece of dough to a 8 inch round and lift each one on to a prepared cookie sheet. Crimp the edges of the dough.

6 Bake in a preheated oven, 375°F, for 15 minutes until lightly golden. Transfer the shortcakes to a wire rack and leave to cool.

7 Mix the cream with the raspberries and spoon on top of one of the shortcakes. Top with the other shortcake round, dust with a little confectioners' sugar and decorate with the extra raspberries and mint leaves.

COOK'S TIP

The shortcake can be made a few days in advance and stored in an airtight container until required.

Plum Cobbler

*This is a favorite dessert which can be adapted to suit
all types of fruit if plums are not available.*

Serves 6

INGREDIENTS

2 lb plums, pits removed and sliced
$^1/_3$ cup superfine sugar
1 tbsp lemon juice

$2^1/_4$ cups all-purpose flour
$^1/_3$ cup granulated sugar
2 tsp baking powder
1 egg, beaten

$^2/_3$ cup buttermilk
$^1/_3$ cup butter, melted and cooled
heavy cream, to serve

1 Lightly grease a 8 cup ovenproof dish.

2 In a large bowl, mix together the plums, superfine sugar, lemon juice, and ¼ cup of the all-purpose flour.

3 Spoon the coated plums into the bottom of the prepared ovenproof dish.

4 Combine the remaining flour, granulated sugar, and baking powder in a bowl.

5 Add the beaten egg, buttermilk and cooled melted butter. Mix everything gently together to form a soft dough.

6 Place spoonfuls of the dough on top of the fruit mixture until it is almost covered.

7 Bake in a preheated oven, 375°F, for about 35-40 minutes until golden brown and bubbling.

8 Serve the pudding very hot, with heavy cream.

COOK'S TIP

*If you cannot find buttermilk, try
using sour cream.*

Blackberry Pudding

A delicious dessert to make when blackberries are in abundance!
If blackberries are unavailable, use other fruits such as currants or gooseberries.

Serves 4

INGREDIENTS

1 lb blackberries
$^1/_3$ cup superfine sugar
1 egg
$^1/_3$ cup soft brown sugar

$^1/_3$ cup butter, melted

8 tbsp milk
$4^1/_2$ oz self-rising flour

1 Lightly grease a large $3^1/_2$ cup ovenproof dish.

2 In a large mixing bowl, gently mix together the blackberries and superfine sugar until well combined.

3 Transfer the blackberry and sugar mixture to the prepared ovenproof dish.

4 Beat the egg and soft brown sugar in a separate mixing bowl. Stir in the melted butter and milk.

5 Sift the flour into the egg and butter mixture and fold together lightly to form a smooth batter.

6 Carefully spread the batter over the blackberry and sugar mixture in the ovenproof dish.

7 Bake the pudding in a preheated oven, 350°F, for about 25-30 minutes until the topping is firm and golden.

8 Sprinkle the pudding with a little sugar and serve hot.

VARIATION

You can add 2 tablespoons of cocoa powder to the batter in step 5, if you prefer a chocolate flavor.

Queen of Puddings

A slightly different version of this old favorite made with the addition of orange rind and marmalade to give a delicious orange flavor.

Serves 8

INGREDIENTS

2¹/₂ cups milk
6 tsp butter
1¹/₄ cups superfine sugar

finely grated rind of 1 orange
4 eggs, separated
³/₄ cup fresh bread crumbs

pinch of salt
6 tbsp orange marmalade

1 Grease a 6 cup ovenproof dish.

2 To make the custard, heat the milk in a pan with the butter, ¼ cup of the superfine sugar, and the grated orange rind until just warm.

3 Whisk the egg yolks in a bowl. Gradually pour the warm milk over the eggs, stirring.

4 Stir the bread crumbs into the pan, then transfer the mixture to the prepared dish and leave to stand for 15 minutes.

5 Bake in a preheated oven, 350°F, for 20-25 minutes until the custard has just set. Remove the custard from the oven but do not turn the oven off.

6 To make the meringue, whisk the egg whites with a pinch of salt until they stand in soft peaks. Whisk in the remaining sugar, a little at a time.

7 Spread the orange marmalade over the cooked custard. Top with the meringue, spreading it right to the edges of the dish.

8 Return the pudding to the oven and bake for a further 20 minutes until the meringue is crisp and golden.

COOK'S TIP

If you prefer a crisper meringue, bake the pudding in the oven for an extra 5 minutes.

Eve's Pudding

*This is a popular family favorite pudding with soft apples
on the bottom and a light buttery sponge on top.*

Serves 6

INGREDIENTS

1 lb cooking apples, peeled, cored,
  and sliced
$^1/_3$ cup granulated sugar
1 tbsp lemon juice
$^1/_3$ cup golden raisins

$^1/_3$ cup butter
$^1/_3$ cup superfine sugar
1 egg, beaten
1$^1/_4$ cups self-rising flour

3 tbsp milk
$^1/_4$ cup slivered almonds
custard or heavy cream,
  to serve

1 Grease an 3½ cup ovenproof dish.

2 Mix the apples with the sugar, lemon juice, and golden raisins. Spoon the mixture into the greased dish.

3 In a bowl, cream the butter and superfine sugar together until pale. Add the egg, a little at a time.

4 Carefully fold in the self-rising flour and stir in the milk to give the mixture a soft, dropping consistency.

5 Spread the mixture over the apples and sprinkle with the slivered almonds.

6 Bake in a preheated oven, 350°F, for 40-45 minutes until the sponge is golden brown.

7 Serve the pudding very hot, accompanied by custard or heavy cream.

COOK'S TIP

To increase the almond flavor of this pudding, add $^1/_4$ cup ground almonds with the flour in step 4.

Bread & Butter Pudding

A traditional pudding full of fruit and spices.
It is the perfect way to use up day-old bread.

Serves 6

INGREDIENTS

7 oz white bread, sliced
10 tsp butter, softened
2 tbsp golden raisins

1 oz candied peel
2 $\frac{1}{2}$ cups milk
4 egg yolks

$\frac{1}{3}$ cup superfine sugar
$\frac{1}{2}$ tsp ground allspice

1 Grease a 5⅓ cup ovenproof dish.

2 Remove the crusts from the bread (optional), spread with butter and cut into quarters.

3 Arrange half of the buttered bread slices in the prepared ovenproof dish. Sprinkle half of the golden raisins and candied peel over the top of the bread.

4 Place the remaining bread slices over the fruit, and then sprinkle over the reserved fruit.

5 To make the custard, bring the milk almost to a boil in a saucepan. Whisk together the egg yolks and the sugar in a bowl, then pour in the warm milk.

6 Strain the warm custard through a strainer. Pour the custard over the bread slices.

7 Leave to stand for 30 minutes, then sprinkle with the ground allspice.

8 Place the ovenproof dish in a roasting pan half-filled with hot water.

9 Bake in a preheated oven, 400°F, for 40-45 minutes until the pudding has just set. Serve warm.

COOK'S TIP

The pudding can be prepared in advance up to step 7 and then set aside until required.

Black Forest Trifle

*Try all the delightful flavors of a Black Forest Gateau
in this new guise – the results are stunning.*

Serves 6-8

INGREDIENTS

6 thin slices chocolate butter cream
  cake
2 x 14 oz can black cherries
2 tbsp kirsch
1 tbsp cornstarch
2 tbsp superfine sugar

$1^3/_4$ cups milk
3 egg yolks
1 egg
$2^3/_4$ oz dark chocolate
$1^1/_4$ cups heavy cream, lightly
  whipped

TO DECORATE:
dark chocolate, melted
maraschino cherries (optional)

1 Place the slices of chocolate
cake in the bottom of a glass
serving bowl.

2 Drain the black cherries,
reserving 6 tbsp of the juice.
Place the cherries and the reserved
juice on top of the cake. Sprinkle
with the kirsch.

3 In a bowl, mix the cornstarch
and superfine sugar. Stir in
enough of the milk to mix to a
smooth paste. Beat in the egg

yolks and the whole egg.

4 Heat the remaining milk in a
small saucepan until almost
boiling, then gradually pour it on
to the egg mixture, whisking well
until it is combined.

5 Place the bowl over a pan of
hot water and cook over a low
heat until the custard thickens,
stirring. Add the chocolate and stir
until melted.

6 Pour the chocolate custard
over the cherries and cool.
When cold, spread the cream over
the custard, swirling with the back
of a spoon. Chill before decorating.

7 To make chocolate caraque,
spread the melted dark
chocolate on a marble or acrylic
board. As it begins to set, pull a
knife through the chocolate at a
45° angle, working quickly.
Remove each caraque as you make
it and chill firmly before using.

Chocolate Charlotte

This chocolate dessert, consisting of a rich chocolate mousse-like filling enclosed in lady's fingers, is a variation of a popular classic.

Serves 8

INGREDIENTS

about 22 lady's fingers
4 tbsp orange-flavored liqueur
9 oz dark chocolate
$^1/_4$ pint heavy cream
4 eggs
$^2/_3$ cup superfine sugar

TO DECORATE:
$^2/_3$ cup whipping cream
2 tbsp superfine sugar
$^1/_2$ tsp vanilla extract
large dark chocolate curls, (see page 50)

chocolate leaves (see page 82) or chocolate shapes (see page 242)

1 Line the base of a Charlotte mold or a deep 7 inch round cake pan with a piece of baking parchment.

2 Place the lady's fingers on a tray and sprinkle with half of the orange-flavored liqueur. Use to line the sides of the mold or pan, trimming if necessary to make a tight fit.

3 Break the chocolate into small pieces, place in a bowl and melt over a pan of hot water.

Remove from the heat and stir in the heavy cream.

4 Separate the eggs and place the whites in a large grease-free bowl. Beat the egg yolks into the chocolate mixture.

5 Whisk the egg whites until standing in stiff peaks, then gradually add the superfine sugar, whisking until stiff and glossy. Carefully fold the egg whites into the chocolate mixture in 2 batches, taking care not to knock out all of

the air. Pour into the center of the mold. Trim the lady's fingers so that they are level with the chocolate mixture. Leave to chill for at least 5 hours.

6 To decorate, whisk the cream, sugar, and vanilla extract until standing in soft peaks. Turn out the Charlotte on to a serving dish. Pipe cream rosettes around the base and decorate with chocolate curls and leaves.

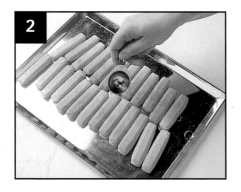

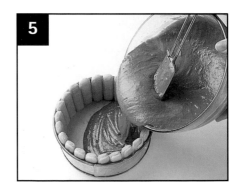

Mississippi Mud Pie

*An all-time favorite with chocoholics — the "mud" refers
to the gooey, rich chocolate layer of the cake.*

Serves 8–10

INGREDIENTS

2 cups all-purpose flour
$^{1}/_{4}$ cup cocoa powder
$^{2}/_{3}$ cup butter
5 tsp superfine sugar
about 2 tbsp cold water

FILLING:
$^{3}/_{4}$ cup butter
12 oz dark muscovado sugar
4 eggs, lightly beaten
4 tbsp cocoa powder, sifted
$5^{1}/_{2}$ oz dark chocolate
$^{1}/_{2}$ pt light cream

1 tsp chocolate extract

TO DECORATE:
$1^{3}/_{4}$ cups heavy cream, whipped
thick bar of chocolate

1 To make the pastry, sift the flour and cocoa powder into a mixing bowl. Rub in the butter until the mixture resembles fine bread crumbs. Stir in the sugar and enough cold water to mix to a soft dough. Chill for 15 minutes.

2 Roll out the dough on a lightly floured surface and use to line a deep 9 inch loose-bottomed flan pan or ceramic flan dish. Line with foil or baking parchment and baking beans. Bake

blind in a preheated oven, 375°F, for 15 minutes. Remove the beans and foil or paper and cook for a further 10 minutes until crisp.

3 To make the filling, beat the butter and sugar in a bowl and gradually beat in the eggs with the cocoa powder. Melt the chocolate and beat it into the mixture with the light cream and the chocolate extract.

4 Pour the mixture into the cooked pie shell and bake at 325°F for 45 minutes or until the filling is set.

5 Leave to cool completely, then transfer the pie to a serving plate, if preferred. Cover with the whipped cream and leave to chill.

6 To make small chocolate curls, use a potato peeler to remove curls from the bar of chocolate. Decorate the pie and leave to chill.

Chocolate Freezer Cake

Hidden in a ring of chocolate cake lies the secret to this freezer cake, a chocolate and mint ice cream. You can use orange or coffee ice cream if preferred.

Serves 8-10

INGREDIENTS

4 eggs
$^3/_4$ cup superfine sugar
$^3/_4$ cup self-rising flour
3 tbsp cocoa powder

$2^1/_4$ cups chocolate and mint ice
  cream
Glossy Chocolate Sauce
  (see page 248)

1 Lightly grease a 9 inch ring pan. Place the eggs and sugar in a large mixing bowl. Using an electric whisk if you have one, whisk the mixture until it is very thick and the whisk leaves a trail. If using a balloon whisk, stand the bowl over a pan of hot water whilst whisking.

2 Sift the flour and cocoa together and fold them into the egg mixture. Pour into the prepared pan and bake in a preheated oven, 350°F, for 30 minutes or until springy to the touch. Leave to cool in the pan before turning out on to a wire rack to cool completely.

3 Rinse the cake pan and line with a strip of plastic wrap, overhanging slightly. Cut the top off the cake about $^1/_2$ inch thick and set aside.

4 Return the cake to the pan. Using a spoon, scoop out the center of the cake leaving a shell about $^1/_2$ inch thick .

5 Remove the ice cream from the freezer and leave to stand for a few minutes, then beat with a wooden spoon until softened a little. Fill the center of the cake with the ice cream, leveling the top. Replace the top of the cake.

6 Cover with the overhanging plastic wrap and freeze for at least 2 hours.

7 To serve, turn the cake out on to a serving dish and drizzle over some of the chocolate sauce in an attractive pattern, if you wish. Cut the cake into slices and serve the remaining sauce separately.

Rich Chocolate Loaf

Another rich chocolate dessert, this loaf is very simple to make and can be served as a tea-time treat as well.

Makes 16 slices

INGREDIENTS

$5\frac{1}{2}$ oz dark chocolate
6 tbsp butter, unsalted
1 x $7\frac{1}{4}$ oz tin condensed milk

2 tsp cinnamon
$2\frac{3}{4}$ oz almonds
$2\frac{3}{4}$ oz amaretti crackers, broken

$1\frac{3}{4}$ oz dried no-need-to-soak
apricots, roughly chopped

1 Line a $1\frac{1}{2}$ lb loaf pan with a sheet of kitchen foil.

2 Using a sharp knife, roughly chop the almonds.

3 Place the chocolate, butter, milk, and cinnamon in a heavy-bottomed saucepan. Heat gently over a low heat for 3–4 minutes, stirring with a wooden spoon, until the chocolate has melted. Beat the mixture well.

4 Stir the almonds, crackers, and apricots into the chocolate mixture in the pan, stirring with a wooden spoon, until well mixed.

5 Pour the mixture into the prepared pan and leave to chill in the refrigerator for about 1 hour or until set.

6 Cut the rich chocolate loaf into slices to serve.

COOK'S TIP

To melt chocolate, first break it into manageable pieces. The smaller the pieces, the quicker it will melt.

COOK'S TIP

When baking or cooking with fat, butter has the finest flavor. If possible, it is best to use unsalted butter as an ingredient in puddings and desserts, unless stated otherwise in the recipe. 'Low-fat' spreads are not suitable for cooking.

Banana & Coconut Cheesecake

The exotic combination of banana and coconut goes well with chocolate as illustrated in this lovely cheesecake. You can use shredded coconut, but fresh coconut will give a better flavor.

Serves 10

INGREDIENTS

8 oz chocolate chip cookies
4 tbsp butter
12 oz medium-fat soft cheese
$1/3$ cup superfine sugar
$1^3/4$ oz fresh coconut, grated
2 tbsp coconut-flavored liqueur
2 ripe bananas

$4^1/2$ oz dark chocolate
1 envelope gelatin
3 tbsp water
$2/3$ cup heavy cream

TO DECORATE:
1 banana
lemon juice
a little melted chocolate

1 Place the cookies in a plastic bag and crush with a rolling pin. Pour into a mixing bowl. Melt the butter and stir into the cookie crumbs until well coated. Firmly press the cookie mixture into the base and up the sides of a 8 inch springform pan.

2 Beat together the soft cheese and superfine sugar until well combined, then beat in the grated coconut and coconut-flavored liqueur. Mash the 2 bananas and beat them in. Melt the dark chocolate and beat in until well combined.

3 Sprinkle the gelatin over the water in a heatproof bowl and leave to go spongy. Place over a pan of hot water and stir until dissolved. Stir into the chocolate mixture. Whisk the cream until just holding its shape and stir into the chocolate mixture. Spoon over the cookie base and chill until set.

4 To serve, carefully transfer to a serving plate. Slice the banana, toss in the lemon juice and arrange around the edge of the cheesecake. Drizzle with melted chocolate and leave to set.

COOK'S TIP

To crack the coconut, pierce 2 of the 'eyes' and drain off the liquid. Tap hard around the center with a hammer until it cracks; lever apart.

Chocolate & Bean Curd Cheesecake

This cheesecake takes a little time to prepare and cook but is well worth the effort.
It is quite rich and is good served or decorated with a little fresh fruit, such as sliced strawberries.

Serves 12

INGREDIENTS

3/4 cup all-purpose flour
3/4 cup ground almonds
3/4 cup brown crystal sugar
10 tbsp vegetarian margarine
1 1/2 lb firm bean curd
3/4 cup vegetable oil
1/2 cup orange juice

3/4 cup brandy
6 tbsp cocoa powder, plus extra to
 decorate
2 tsp almond extract
confectioners' sugar and Cape
 gooseberries, to decorate

1 Put the flour, ground almonds, and 1 tablespoon of the sugar in a bowl and mix well. Rub the margarine into the mixture to form a dough.

2 Lightly grease and line the base of a 9 inch spring-form pan. Press the dough into the base of the pan to cover, pushing the dough right up to the edge of the pan.

3 Roughly chop the bean curd and put in a food processor with all of the remaining ingredients and blend until smooth and creamy. Pour over the base in the pan and cook in a preheated oven, 325°F, for 1–1 1/4 hours or until set.

4 Leave to cool in the pan for 5 minutes, then remove and chill in the refrigerator. Dust with confectioners' sugar and cocoa powder. Decorate and serve.

COOK'S TIP

Cape gooseberries make an attractive decoration for many desserts. Peel open the papery husks to expose the bright orange fruits.

Marble Cheesecake

*A dark and white chocolate cheesecake filling is marbled together
to a give an attractive finish to this rich and decadent dessert.*

Serves 10-12

INGREDIENTS

BASE:
8 oz toasted oat cereal
$^1/_2$ cup toasted hazelnuts, chopped
4 tbsp butter
1 oz dark chocolate

FILLING:
12 oz full fat soft cheese
7 tbsp superfine sugar
$^3/_4$ cup thick yogurt
$1^1/_4$ cups heavy cream

1 envelope gelatin
3 tbsp water
6 oz dark chocolate, melted
6 oz white chocolate, melted

1 Place the toasted oat cereal in a plastic bag and crush with a rolling pin. Pour the crushed cereal into a mixing bowl and stir in the hazelnuts.

2 Melt the butter and chocolate together over a low heat and stir into the cereal mixture, stirring until well coated.

3 Using the bottom of a glass, press the mixture into the base and up the sides of a 8 inch springform pan.

4 Beat together the cheese and sugar with a wooden spoon until smooth. Beat in the yogurt. Whip the cream until just holding its shape and fold into the mixture. Sprinkle the gelatin over the water in a heatproof bowl and leave to go spongy. Place over a pan of hot water and stir until dissolved. Stir into the mixture.

5 Divide the mixture in half and beat the dark chocolate into one half and the white chocolate into the other half.

6 Place alternate spoonfuls of mixture on top of the cereal base. Swirl the filling together with the tip of a knife to give a marbled effect. Level the top with a scraper or a spatula. Leave to chill until set before serving.

COOK'S TIP

For a lighter texture, fold in 2 egg whites whipped to soft peaks before folding in the cream in step 4.

White Chocolate Ice Cream in a Cookie Cup

This white chocolate ice cream is served in a cookie cup.
If liked, top with a chocolate sauce for a true addict's treat.

Serves 6

INGREDIENTS

ICE CREAM:
1 egg
1 egg yolk
3 tbsp superfine sugar
5$\frac{1}{2}$ oz white chocolate

1$\frac{1}{4}$ cups milk
$\frac{2}{3}$ cup heavy cream

COOKIE CUPS:
1 egg white
4 tbsp superfine sugar
2 tbsp all-purpose flour, sifted
2 tbsp cocoa powder, sifted
2 tbsp butter, melted

1 Place baking parchment on 2 baking sheets. To make the ice cream, beat the egg, egg yolks, and sugar. Break the chocolate into pieces, place in a bowl with 3 tbsp milk and melt over a pan of hot water. Heat the milk until almost boiling and pour on to the eggs, whisking. Place over a pan of simmering water and cook, stirring until the mixture thickens enough to coat the back of a wooden spoon. Whisk in the chocolate. Cover with dampened baking parchment and let cool.

2 Whip the cream until just holding its shape and fold into the custard. Transfer to a freezer container and freeze the mixture for 1-2 hours until frozen 1 inch from the sides. Scrape into a bowl and beat again until smooth. Re-freeze until firm.

3 To make the cups, beat the egg white and sugar together. Beat in the flour and cocoa, then the butter. Place 1 tbsp of mixture on one sheet; spread out to a 5 inch circle. Bake in a preheated oven, 400°F, for 4-5 minutes. Remove and mold over an upturned cup. Leave to set, then cool on a wire rack. Repeat to make 6 cups. Serve the ice cream in the cups.

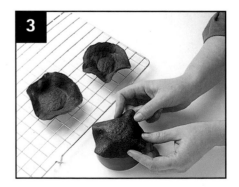

Frosted White Chocolate Terrine

This frosted dessert is somewhere between a chocolate mousse and an ice cream.
Serve it with a chocolate sauce or a fruit coulis and fresh fruit.

Serves 8-10

INGREDIENTS

2 tbsp granulated sugar
5 tbsp water

$10^1/_2$ oz white chocolate
3 eggs, separated

$1^1/_4$ cups heavy cream

1 Line a 1 lb loaf pan with foil or plastic wrap, pressing out as many creases as you can.

2 Place the granulated sugar and water in a heavy-bottomed pan and heat gently, stirring until the sugar has dissolved. Bring to a boil and boil for 1-2 minutes until syrupy, then remove the pan from the heat.

3 Break the white chocolate into small pieces and stir it into the syrup, continuing to stir until the chocolate has melted and combined with the syrup. Leave to cool slightly.

4 Beat the egg yolks into the chocolate mixture. Leave to cool completely.

5 Lightly whip the cream until just holding its shape and fold it into the chocolate mixture.

6 Whisk the egg whites in a grease-free bowl until they are standing in soft peaks. Fold into the chocolate mixture. Pour into the prepared loaf pan and freeze overnight.

7 To serve, remove from the freezer about 10-15 minutes before serving. Turn out of the pan and cut into slices to serve.

COOK'S TIP

To make a coulis, place 8 oz soft fruit of your choice – strawberries, black or red currants, mango, or raspberries are ideal – in a food processor or blender. Add 1-2 tbsp confectioners' sugar and blend to form a purée. If the fruit contains seeds, push the purée through a strainer to remove them. Leave to chill until required.

Layered Chocolate Mousse

Three layers of fabulous rich mousse give this elegant dessert extra chocolate appeal. It is a little fiddly to prepare, but well worth the extra effort.

Serves 8

INGREDIENTS

3 eggs
1 tsp cornstarch
4 tbsp superfine sugar
1¼ cups milk
1 envelope gelatin

3 tbsp water
1¼ cups heavy cream
2¾ oz dark chocolate
2¾ oz white chocolate
2¾ oz milk chocolate

chocolate caraque, to decorate (see page 218)

1 Line a 1 lb loaf pan with baking parchment. Separate the eggs, putting each egg white in a separate bowl. Place the egg yolks and sugar in a large mixing bowl and whisk until well combined. Place the milk in a pan and heat gently, stirring until almost boiling. Pour the milk on to the egg yolks, whisking.

2 Set the bowl over a pan of gently simmering water and cook, stirring until the mixture thickens enough to thinly coat the back of a wooden spoon.

3 Sprinkle the gelatin over the water in a small heatproof bowl and leave to go spongy. Place over a pan of hot water and stir until dissolved. Stir into the hot mixture. Leave to cool.

4 Whip the cream until just holding its shape. Fold into the egg custard, then divide the mixture into 3. Melt the 3 types of chocolate separately. Fold the dark chocolate into one egg custard portion. Whisk one egg white until standing in soft peaks and fold into the dark chocolate custard until

combined. Pour into the prepared pan and level the top. Chill in the coldest part of the refrigerator until just set. Leave the remaining mixtures at room temperature.

5 Fold the white chocolate into another portion of the egg custard. Whisk another egg white and fold in. Pour on top of the dark chocolate layer and chill quickly. Repeat with the remaining milk chocolate and egg white. Chill until set. To serve, carefully turn out on to a serving dish and decorate with chocolate caraque.

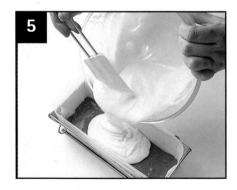

Mocha Creams

These creamy chocolate and coffee-flavored desserts
make a perfect end to a fine meal.

Serves 4

INGREDIENTS

8 oz dark chocolate
1 tbsp instant coffee
1¼ cups boiling water
1 envelope gelatin
3 tbsp cold water

1 tsp vanilla extract
1 tbsp coffee-flavored liqueur
 (optional)

1¼ cups heavy cream
4 chocolate coffee beans
8 amaretti cookies

1 Break the chocolate into small pieces and place in a saucepan with the coffee. Stir in the boiling water and heat gently, stirring until the chocolate melts.

2 Sprinkle the gelatin over the cold water and leave to go spongy, then whisk it into the hot chocolate mixture to dissolve it.

3 Stir in the vanilla extract and coffee-flavored liqueur, if using. Leave to stand in a cool place until just beginning to thicken; whisk from time to time.

4 Whisk the cream until it is standing in soft peaks, then reserve a little for decorating the desserts and fold the remainder into the chocolate mixture. Spoon into serving dishes and leave to set.

5 Decorate with the reserved cream and coffee beans and serve with the cookies.

COOK'S TIP

If preferred, the puddings can be made in one large serving dish.

VARIATION

To add a delicious almond flavor to the dessert, replace the coffee-flavored liqueur with almond-flavored liqueur.

Chocolate & Vanilla Creams

These rich, creamy desserts are completely irresistible.
Serve them with crisp dessert cookies.

Serves 4

INGREDIENTS

2 cups heavy cream
$1/3$ cup superfine sugar
1 vanilla pod
$3/4$ cup crème fraîche
2 tsp gelatin

3 tbsp water
$1^3/4$ oz dark chocolate

MARBLED CHOCOLATE SHAPES:
a little melted white chocolate
a little melted dark chocolate

1 Place the cream and sugar in a saucepan. Cut the vanilla pod into 2 pieces and add to the cream. Heat gently, stirring until the sugar has dissolved, then bring to a boil. Reduce the heat and leave to simmer for 2-3 minutes.

2 Remove the pan from the heat and take out the vanilla pod. Stir in the crème fraîche.

3 Sprinkle the gelatin over the water in a small heatproof bowl and leave to go spongy, then place over a pan of hot water and

stir until dissolved. Stir into the cream mixture. Pour half of this mixture into another mixing bowl.

4 Melt the dark chocolate and stir it into one half of the cream mixture. Pour the chocolate mixture into 4 individual glass serving dishes and chill for 15-20 minutes until just set. While it is chilling, keep the vanilla mixture at room temperature.

5 Spoon the vanilla mixture on top of the chocolate mixture and chill until the vanilla is set.

6 Meanwhile, make the shapes for the decoration. Spoon the melted white chocolate into a paper pastry bag and snip off the tip. Spread some melted dark chocolate on a piece of baking parchment. Whilst still wet, pipe a fine line of white chocolate in a scribble over the top. Use the tip of a toothpick to marble the white chocolate into the dark. When firm but not too hard, cut into shapes with a small shaped cutter or a sharp knife. Chill the shapes until firm, then use to decorate the desserts.

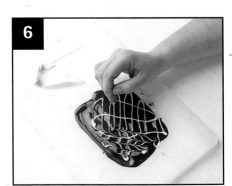

Chocolate Zabaglione

As light as air with a creamy texture, this sophisticated dessert is sure to be a real winner. As it only uses a little chocolate, choose one with a minimum of 70 per cent cocoa solids for a good flavor.

Serves 2

INGREDIENTS

4 egg yolks
4 tbsp superfine sugar
1³/₄ oz dark chocolate

1 cup Marsala wine
cocoa powder, to dust

1 In a large glass mixing bowl, whisk together the egg yolks and superfine sugar until you have a very pale mixture, using electric beaters.

2 Grate the chocolate finely and fold into the egg mixture. Fold in the wine.

3 Place the mixing bowl over a saucepan of gently simmering water and set the beaters on the lowest speed or swop to a balloon whisk. Cook gently, whisking continuously until the mixture thickens; take care not to overcook or the mixture will curdle.

4 Spoon the hot mixture into warmed individual glass dishes and dust lightly with cocoa powder. Serve the zabaglione as soon as possible so that it is warm, light and fluffy.

COOK'S TIP

Make the dessert just before serving as the mixture will separate if left to stand. If it begins to curdle, you may be able to save it if you remove it from the heat immediately and place it in a bowl of cold water to stop the cooking. Whisk furiously until the mixture comes together.

COOK'S TIP

For an up-to-the minute serving idea, spoon the zabaglione into coffee cups and serve with amaretti biscuits to the side of the saucer.

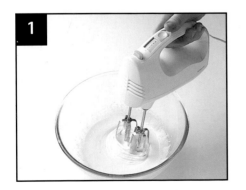

Chocolate Meringue Pie

Crumbly cracker base, rich creamy chocolate filling topped with fluffy meringue – what could be more indulgent than this fabulous dessert?

Serves 6

INGREDIENTS

8 oz dark chocolate graham crackers
4 tbsp butter

FILLING:
3 egg yolks
4 tbsp superfine sugar

4 tbsp cornstarch
2¹/₂ cups milk
3¹/₂ oz dark chocolate, melted

MERINGUE:
2 egg whites
7 tbsp superfine sugar
¹/₄ tsp vanilla extract

1 Place the graham crackers in a plastic bag and crush with a rolling pin. Pour into a mixing bowl. Melt the butter and stir it into the cracker crumbs until well mixed. Press the cracker mixture firmly into the base and up the sides of a 9 inch flan pan or dish.

2 To make the filling, beat the egg yolks, superfine sugar, and cornstarch in a large bowl until they form a smooth paste, adding a little of the milk if necessary. Heat the milk until almost boiling, then slowly pour it on to the egg mixture, whisking well.

3 Return the mixture to the saucepan and cook gently, whisking constantly until it thickens. Remove from the heat. Whisk in the melted chocolate, then pour it on to the graham cracker base.

4 To make the meringue, whisk the egg whites in a large mixing bowl until standing in soft peaks. Gradually whisk in about two-thirds of the sugar until the mixture is stiff and glossy. Fold in the remaining sugar and vanilla extract.

5 Spread the meringue over the filling, swirling the surface with the back of a spoon to give it an attractive finish. Bake in a preheated oven, 375°F, for 30 minutes or until the meringue is golden. Serve hot or just warm.

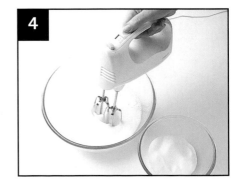

Chocolate Pear & Almond Flan

This attractive dessert consists of a flan filled with pears cooked in a chocolate, almond-flavored sponge. It is delicious served hot or cold.

Serves 6

INGREDIENTS

³/₄ cup all-purpose flour
¹/₄ cup ground almonds
¹/₄ cup block margarine
about 3 tbsp water

FILLING:
14 oz can pear halves, in
    unsweetened juice
4 tbsp butter
4 tbsp superfine sugar

2 eggs, beaten
1 cup ground almonds
2 tbsp cocoa powder
few drops of almond extract
confectioners' sugar, to dust

CHOCOLATE SAUCE:
4 tbsp superfine sugar
3 tbsp light corn syrup

¹/₃ cup water
6 oz dark chocolate, broken into
    pieces
2 tbsp butter

1 Lightly grease a 8 inch flan pan. Sift the flour into a mixing bowl and stir in the almonds. Rub in the margarine with your fingertips until the mixture resembles bread crumbs. Add enough water to mix to a soft dough. Cover, chill in the freezer for 10 minutes, then roll out and use to line the pan. Prick the base and chill.

2 To make the filling, drain the pears well. Beat the butter and sugar until light and fluffy. Beat in the eggs. Fold in the almonds, cocoa powder and extract. Spread the chocolate mixture in the pie shell and arrange the pears on top, pressing down lightly. Bake in the center of a preheated oven, 400°F, for 30 minutes or until the filling has risen. Cool slightly and transfer to a serving dish, if wished. Dust with sugar.

3 To make the sauce, place the sugar, syrup, and water in a pan and heat gently, stirring until the sugar dissolves. Boil gently for 1 minute. Remove from the heat, add the chocolate and butter and stir until melted. Serve with the flan.

Pecan & Chocolate Fudge Ring

*Although this can be served cold as a cake, it is
absolutely delicious served hot as a pudding.*

Serves 6

INGREDIENTS

FUDGE SAUCE:
3 tbsp butter
3 tbsp light muscovado sugar
4 tbsp light corn syrup
2 tbsp milk
1 tbsp cocoa powder
1 1/2 oz dark chocolate

1 3/4 oz pecan nuts, finely chopped

CAKE:
generous 1/3 cup soft margarine
7 tbsp light muscovado sugar
1 cup self-rising flour
2 eggs

2 tbsp milk
1 tbsp light corn syrup

1 Lightly grease a 8 inch ring pan.

2 To make the fudge sauce, place the butter, sugar, syrup, milk, and cocoa powder in a small pan and heat gently, keep stirring until combined.

3 Break the chocolate into pieces, add to the mixture and stir until melted. Stir in the chopped nuts. Pour into the base of the pan and leave to cool.

4 To make the cake, place all of the ingredients in a mixing bowl and beat until smooth. Carefully spoon the cake mixture over the chocolate fudge sauce.

5 Bake in a preheated oven, 350°F, for 35 minutes or until the cake is springy to the touch.

6 Leave to cool in the pan for 5 minutes, then turn out on to a serving dish and serve.

COOK'S TIP

To make in the microwave, place the butter, sugar, syrup, milk, and cocoa powder for the sauce in a microwave-proof bowl. Cook on High for 2 minutes, stirring twice. Stir in the chocolate until melted, then add the nuts. Pour into a 5 cup microwave-proof ring mold. Make the cake and cook on High for 3-4 minutes until just dry on top; stand for 5 minutes.

Chocolate Fudge Pudding

This fabulous steamed pudding, served with a rich chocolate fudge sauce, is perfect for cold winter days – and it can be made in double quick time in the microwave, if you have one.

Serves 6

INGREDIENTS

generous $^1/_3$ cup soft margarine
$1^1/_4$ cups self-rising flour
$^1/_2$ cup light corn syrup
3 eggs
$^1/_4$ cup cocoa powder

CHOCOLATE FUDGE SAUCE:
$3^1/_2$ oz dark chocolate
$^1/_2$ cup sweetened condensed milk
4 tbsp heavy cream

1 Lightly grease a 5 cup mixing bowl.

2 Place the ingredients for the sponge in a mixing bowl and beat until well combined and smooth.

3 Spoon into the prepared bowl and level the top. Cover with a disc of baking parchment and tie a pleated sheet of foil over the basin. Steam for $1^1/_2$-2 hours until the pudding is cooked and springy to the touch.

4 To make the sauce, break the chocolate into small pieces and place in a small pan with the condensed milk. Heat gently, stirring until the chocolate melts.

5 Remove the pan from the heat and stir in the heavy cream.

6 To serve the pudding, turn it out on to a serving plate and pour over a little of the chocolate fudge sauce. Serve the remaining sauce separately.

COOK'S TIP

To cook the cake in the microwave, cook it, uncovered, on High for 4 minutes, turning the basin once. Leave to stand for at least 5 minutes before turning out. While the pudding is standing, make the sauce. Break the chocolate into pieces and place in a microwave-proof bowl with the milk. Cook on High for 1 minute, then stir until the chocolate melts. Stir in the heavy cream and serve.

Chocolate Fruit Crumble

A popular dessert, the addition of chocolate in the topping makes it even more of a treat.
A good way of enticing children to eat a fruit dessert.

Serves 4

INGREDIENTS

14 oz can apricots, in unsweetened juice

1 lb cooking apples, peeled and sliced thickly

³/₄ cup all-purpose flour

¹/₃ cup butter

²/₃ cup oatmeal

4 tbsp superfine sugar

²/₃ cup chocolate chips

1 Lightly grease an ovenproof dish with a small amount of butter or margarine.

2 Drain the apricots, reserving 4 tbsp of the juice. Place the apples and apricots in the prepared ovenproof dish with the reserved apricot juice and toss to mix.

3 Sift the flour into a mixing bowl. Cut the butter into small cubes and rub in with your fingertips until the mixture resembles fine bread crumbs. Stir in the oatmeal, sugar, and chocolate chips.

4 Sprinkle the crumble mixture over the apples and apricots and level the top roughly. Do not press the crumble into the fruit.

5 Bake in a preheated oven, 180°C, for 40-45 minutes or until the topping is golden. Serve hot or cold.

COOK'S TIP

You can use dark, milk or white chocolate chips in this recipe or a mixture of all three.

VARIATION

Other fruits can be used to make this crumble – fresh pears mixed with fresh or frozen raspberries work well. If you do not use canned fruit, add 4 tablespoons of orange juice to the fresh fruit.

VARIATION

For a double chocolate crumble, replace 1-2 tablespoons of flour with cocoa powder.

Saucy Chocolate Pudding

*In this recipe, the mixture separates out during cooking to produce a cream sponge
topping and a delicious chocolate sauce on the bottom.*

Serves 4

INGREDIENTS

1¹/₄ cups milk
2³/₄ oz dark chocolate
¹/₂ tsp vanilla extract
7 tbsp superfine sugar
generous ¹/₃ cup butter
1¹/₄ cups self-rising flour

2 tbsp cocoa powder
confectioners' sugar, to dust

FOR THE SAUCE:
3 tbsp cocoa powder
4 tbsp light muscovado sugar
1¹/₄ cups boiling water

1 Lightly grease an 3³/₄ cup ovenproof dish.

2 Place the milk in a small pan. Break the chocolate into pieces and add to the milk. Heat gently, stirring until the chocolate melts. Leave to cool slightly. Stir in the vanilla extract.

3 Beat together the superfine sugar and butter in a bowl until light and fluffy. Sift the flour and cocoa powder together. Add to the bowl with the chocolate milk and beat until smooth, using an electric whisk if you have one. Pour the mixture into the prepared dish.

4 To make the sauce, mix together the cocoa powder and sugar. Add a little boiling water and mix to a smooth paste, then stir in the remaining water. Pour the sauce over the pudding but do not mix in.

5 Place the dish on to a baking sheet and bake in a preheated oven, 350°F, for 40 minutes or until dry on top and springy to the touch. Leave to stand for about 5 minutes, then dust with a little confectioners' sugar just before serving.

VARIATION

For a mocha sauce, add 1 tbsp instant coffee to the cocoa powder and sugar in step 4, before mixing to a paste with the boiling water.

Chocolate Apple Pie

Easy-to-make crumbly chocolate pastry encases a delicious apple filling studded with chocolate chips. This recipe is guaranteed to become a firm family favorite.

Serves 6

INGREDIENTS

CHOCOLATE PASTRY:
4 tbsp cocoa powder
1³/4 cups all-purpose flour
2 egg yolks
³/4 cup softened butter
4 tbsp superfine sugar
few drops of vanilla extract
cold water, to mix

FILLING:
1 lb 10 oz cooking apples
2 tbsp butter
¹/2 tsp ground cinnamon
³/4 cup dark chocolate chips
a little egg white, beaten
¹/2 tsp superfine sugar

whipped cream or vanilla ice cream,
to serve

1 To make the pastry, sift the cocoa powder and flour into a mixing bowl and rub in the butter until the mixture resembles fine bread crumbs. Stir in the sugar. Add the egg yolk, vanilla extract, and enough water to mix to a dough.

2 Roll out the dough on a lightly floured surface and use to line a deep 8 inch flan or cake pan. Chill for 30 minutes.

Roll out any trimmings and cut out some pastry leaves to decorate the top of the pie.

3 Peel, core, and thickly slice the apples. Place half of the apple slices in a saucepan with the butter and cinnamon and cook over a gently heat, until the apples soften.

4 Stir in the uncooked apple slices, leave to cool slightly,

then stir in the chocolate chips. Prick the base of the pie shell and pile the apple mixture into it. Arrange the pastry leaves on top. Brush the leaves with a little egg white and sprinkle with superfine sugar.

5 Bake in a preheated oven, 350°F, for 35 minutes until the pastry is crisp. Serve warm or cold, with whipped cream or vanilla ice cream.

Chocolate & Banana Pancakes

Pancakes are given the chocolate treatment to make a rich and fabulous dessert to round off a dinner party. Prepare this recipe ahead of time for trouble-free entertaining.

Serves 4

INGREDIENTS

3 large bananas
6 tbsp orange juice
grated rind of 1 orange
2 tbsp orange- or banana-flavored
  liqueur

HOT CHOCOLATE SAUCE:
1 tbsp cocoa powder

2 tsp cornstarch
3 tbsp milk
1^1/$_2$ oz dark chocolate
1 tbsp butter
^{1}/$_2$ cup light corn syrup
^{1}/$_4$ tsp vanilla extract

PANCAKES:
1 cup all-purpose flour
1 tbsp cocoa powder
1 egg
1 tsp sunflower oil
1^1/$_4$ cups milk
oil, for frying

1 Peel and slice the bananas and arrange them in a dish with the orange juice and rind and the liqueur. Set aside.

2 Mix the cocoa powder and cornstarch in a bowl, then stir in the milk. Break the dark chocolate into pieces and place in a pan with the butter and light corn syrup. Heat gently, stirring until well blended. Add the cocoa mixture and bring to a boil over a

gentle heat, stirring. Simmer for 1 minute, then remove from the heat and stir in the vanilla extract.

3 To make the pancakes, sift the flour and cocoa into a mixing bowl and make a well in the center. Add the egg and oil. Gradually whisk in the milk to form a smooth batter. Heat a little oil in a heavy-based skillet and pour off any excess. Pour in a little batter and tilt the pan to coat the

base. Cook over a medium heat until the underside is browned. Flip over and cook the other side. Slide the pancake out of the pan and keep warm. Repeat until all the batter has been used.

4 To serve, reheat the chocolate sauce for 1-2 minutes. Fill the pancakes with the bananas and fold in half or into triangles. Pour over a little chocolate sauce and serve.

Chocolate Apple Pancake Stack

If you cannot wait to get your first chocolate 'fix' of the day, serve these pancakes for breakfast. They also make a perfect family dessert.

Serves 4–6

INGREDIENTS

2 cups all-purpose flour
1 1/2 tsp baking powder
4 tbsp superfine sugar
1 egg
1 tbsp butter, melted

1 1/4 cups milk
1 eating apple
1 3/4 oz dark chocolate chips
Hot Chocolate Sauce (see page 260)
    or maple syrup, to serve

1 Sift the flour and baking powder into a mixing bowl. Stir in the superfine sugar. Make a well in the center and add the egg and melted butter. Gradually whisk in the milk to form a smooth batter.

2 Peel, core, and grate the apple and stir it into the batter with the chocolate chips.

3 Heat a griddle or heavy-based skillet over a medium heat and grease it lightly. For each pancake, place about 2 tablespoons of the batter on to the griddle or skillet and spread to make a 3 inch round.

4 Cook for a few minutes until you see bubbles appear on the surface of the pancake. Turn over and cook for a further 1 minute. Remove from the skillet and keep warm. Repeat with the remaining batter to make about 12 pancakes.

5 To serve, stack 2 or 3 pancakes on an individual serving plate and serve with the hot chocolate sauce or maple syrup.

COOK'S TIP

To keep the cooked pancakes warm, pile them on top of each other with baking parchment in between to prevent them sticking to each other.

VARIATION

Milk chocolate chips can be used instead of the dark ones, if preferred.

Chocolate Hazelnut Pots

Chocoholics will adore these creamy desserts consisting of a rich baked chocolate custard with the delicious flavor of hazelnuts.

Serves 6

INGREDIENTS

2 eggs
2 egg yolks
1 tbsp superfine sugar

1 tsp cornstarch
2$\frac{1}{2}$ cups milk
3 oz dark chocolate
4 tbsp chocolate and hazelnut spread

TO DECORATE:
grated chocolate or large chocolate curls (see page 50)

1 Beat together the eggs, egg yolks, superfine sugar, and cornstarch until well combined. Heat the milk until almost boiling.

2 Gradually pour the milk on to the eggs, whisking as you do so. Melt the chocolate and hazelnut spread in a bowl set over a pan of gently simmering water, then whisk the melted chocolate mixture into the eggs.

3 Pour into 6 small ovenproof dishes and cover the dishes with foil. Place them in a roasting pan. Fill the pan with boiling water to come halfway up the sides of the dishes.

4 Bake in a preheated oven, 325°F, for 35-40 minutes until the custard is just set. Remove from the pan and cool, then chill until required. Serve decorated with grated chocolate or chocolate curls.

COOK'S TIP

The foil lid prevents a skin forming on the surface of the custards.

COOK'S TIP

This dish is traditionally made in little pots called pots de crème, *which are individual ovenproof dishes with a lid. Ramekins are fine. The dessert can also be made in one large dish; cook for about 1 hour or until set.*

Chocolate Mint Swirl

*The classic combination of chocolate and mint flavors makes
an attractive dessert for special occasions.*

Serves 6

INGREDIENTS

1¹/₄ cups heavy cream
²/₃ cup creamy fromage blanc
2 tbsp confectioners' sugar
1 tbsp crème de menthe

6 oz dark chocolate
chocolate, to decorate

1 Place the cream in a large mixing bowl and whisk until standing in soft peaks.

2 Fold in the fromage blanc and confectioners' sugar, then place about one-third of the mixture in a smaller bowl. Stir the crème de menthe into the smaller bowl. Melt the dark chocolate and stir it into the remaining mixture.

3 Place alternate spoonfuls of the 2 mixtures into serving glasses, then swirl the mixture together to give a decorative effect. Leave to chill until required.

4 To make the piped chocolate decorations, melt a small amount of chocolate and place in a paper pastry bag.

5 Place a sheet of baking parchment on a board and pipe squiggles, stars or flower shapes with the melted chocolate. Alternatively, to make curved decorations, pipe decorations on to a long strip of baking parchment, then carefully place the strip over a rolling pin, securing with sticky tape. Leave the chocolate to set, then carefully remove from the baking parchment.

6 Decorate each dessert with piped chocolate decorations and serve. Alternatively, the desserts can be decorated and then chilled, if preferred.

COOK'S TIP

*Pipe the patterns freehand or draw
patterns on to baking parchment
first, turn the parchment over
and then pipe the chocolate,
following the drawn outline.*

Rich Chocolate Ice Cream

A rich flavored chocolate ice cream which is delicious served on its own or with a chocolate sauce. For a special dessert, serve in these attractive trellis cups.

Serves 6-8

INGREDIENTS

ICE CREAM:
1 egg
3 egg yolks
6 tbsp superfine sugar
1$\frac{1}{4}$ cups full cream milk

9 oz dark chocolate
1$\frac{1}{4}$ cups heavy cream

TRELLIS CUPS:
3$\frac{1}{2}$ oz dark chocolate

1 Beat together the egg, egg yolks, and superfine sugar in a mixing bowl until well combined. Heat the milk until almost boiling.

2 Gradually pour the hot milk on to the eggs, whisking as you do so. Place the bowl over a pan of gently simmering water and cook, stirring until the mixture thickens sufficiently to thinly coat the back of a wooden spoon.

3 Break the dark chocolate into small pieces and add to the

hot custard. Stir until the chocolate has melted. Cover with a sheet of dampened baking parchment and leave to cool.

4 Whip the cream until just holding its shape, then fold into the cooled chocolate custard. Transfer to a freezer container and freeze for 1-2 hours until the mixture is frozen 1 inch from the sides.

5 Scrape the ice cream into a chilled bowl and beat again until smooth. Re-freeze until firm.

6 To make the trellis cups, invert a muffin pan and cover 6 alternate mounds with plastic wrap. Melt the chocolate, place it in a paper pastry bag and snip off the end.

7 Pipe a circle around the base of the mound, then pipe chocolate back and forth over it to form a trellis; carefully pipe a double thickness. Pipe around the base again. Chill until set, then lift from the pan and remove the plastic wrap. Serve the ice cream in the trellis cups.

Baked Chocolate Alaska

A cool dessert that leaves the cook completely unflustered. Light meringue tops chocolate ice cream
for this divine dessert – you can assemble it in advance and pop into the freezer until required.

Serves 6

INGREDIENTS

2 eggs
4 tbsp superfine sugar
generous ¼ cup all-purpose flour
2 tbsp cocoa powder
3 egg whites

²/₃ cup superfine sugar
4½ cups good quality chocolate ice
cream

1 Grease an 7 inch round cake pan and line the base with baking parchment.

2 Whisk the egg and the 4 tbsp sugar in a mixing bowl until very thick and pale. Sift the flour and cocoa powder together and carefully fold in.

3 Pour into the prepared pan and bake in a preheated oven, 425°F, for 7 minutes or until springy to the touch. Transfer to a wire rack to cool completely.

4 Whisk the egg whites in a grease-free bowl until they are standing in soft peaks. Gradually add the sugar, whisking until you have a thick, glossy meringue.

5 Place the sponge on a baking sheet and pile the ice cream on to the center in a heaped dome.

6 Pipe or spread the meringue over the ice cream, making sure the ice cream is completely enclosed. (At this point the dessert can be frozen, if wished.)

7 Return it to the oven, for 5 minutes until the meringue is just golden. Serve immediately.

COOK'S TIP

This dessert is delicious served with a blackcurrant coulis. Cook a few blackcurrants in a little orange juice until soft, purée and push through a strainer, then sweeten to taste with a little confectioners' sugar.

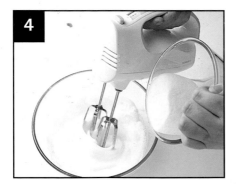

White Chocolate & Almond Tart

*This is a variation on the classic pecan pie recipe – here nuts
and chocolate are encased in a thick syrup filling.*

Serves 8

INGREDIENTS

PASTRY:
1¼ cups all-purpose flour
5 tsp superfine sugar
½ cup butter, cut into small pieces
1 tbsp water

FILLING:
½ cup light corn syrup
1¾ oz butter
⅓ cup soft brown sugar
3 eggs, lightly beaten

½ cup whole blanched almonds,
　roughly chopped
3½ oz white chocolate, chopped
　roughly
cream, to serve (optional)

1 To make the pastry, place the flour and sugar in a mixing bowl and rub in the butter with your fingers. Add the water and work the mixture together until a soft pastry has formed. Wrap and leave to chill for 30 minutes.

2 On a lightly floured surface, roll out the dough and line a 9½ inch loose-bottomed flan pan. Prick the pastry with a fork and leave to chill for 30 minutes. Line the pie shell with foil and baking beans and bake in a preheated oven, 375°F, for 15 minutes. Remove the foil and baking beans and cook for a further 15 minutes.

3 To make the filling, gently melt the syrup, butter, and sugar together in a saucepan. Remove from the heat and leave to cool slightly. Stir in the beaten eggs, almonds, and chocolate.

4 Pour the chocolate and nut filling into the prepared pie shell and cook in the oven for 30–35 minutes or until just set. Leave to cool before removing the tart from the pan. Serve with cream, if wished.

VARIATION

You can use a mixture of white and dark chocolate for this tart, if preferred.

Sticky Chocolate Pudding

These individual puddings always look impressive at the end of a meal.

Serves 6

INGREDIENTS

$^1/_2$ cup butter, softened
$^3/_4$ cup soft brown sugar
3 eggs, beaten
pinch of salt
1 oz cocoa powder

1 cup self-rising flour
1 oz dark chocolate, chopped finely
$2^3/_4$ oz white chocolate, chopped
  finely

SAUCE:
$^2/_3$ cup heavy cream
$^1/_3$ cup soft brown sugar
6 tsp butter

1 Lightly grease 6 individual $^3/_4$ cup molds.

2 In a bowl, cream together the butter and sugar until pale and fluffy. Beat in the eggs a little at a time, beating well after each addition.

3 Sift the salt, cocoa powder, and flour into the creamed mixture and fold through the mixture. Stir the chopped chocolate into the mixture until evenly combined.

4 Divide the mixture between the prepared molds. Lightly grease 6 squares of foil and use them to cover the tops of the molds. Press around the edges to seal.

5 Place the molds in a roasting pan and pour in boiling water to come halfway up the sides of the molds.

6 Bake in a preheated oven, 350°F, for 50 minutes, or until a skewer inserted into the center comes out clean.

7 Remove the molds from the roasting pan and set aside while you prepare the sauce.

8 To make the sauce, put the cream, sugar, and butter into a pan and bring to a boil over a gentle heat. Simmer gently until the sugar has dissolved.

9 To serve, run a knife around the edge of each pudding, then turn out on to serving plates. Pour the sauce over the top of the puddings and serve immediately.

Chocolate Brownie Roulade

The addition of nuts and raisins has given this dessert extra texture,
making it similar to that of chocolate brownies.

Serves 8

INGREDIENTS

5¹/₂ oz dark chocolate, broken into
   pieces
3 tbsp water
³/₄ cup superfine sugar
5 eggs, separated

2 tbsp raisins, chopped
1 oz pecan nuts, chopped
pinch of salt

1¹/₄ cups heavy cream, whipped
   lightly
confectioners' sugar, for dusting

1 Grease a 12 x 8 inch jelly-roll pan and line with baking parchment, grease the parchment.

2 Melt the chocolate with the water in a small saucepan over a low heat until the chocolate has just melted. Leave to cool.

3 In a bowl, whisk the sugar and egg yolks for 2-3 minutes with a hand-held electric whisk until thick and pale.

4 Fold in the cooled chocolate, raisins, and pecan nuts.

5 In a separate bowl, whisk the egg whites with the salt. Fold one quarter of the egg whites into the chocolate mixture, then fold in the rest of the whites, working lightly and quickly.

6 Transfer the mixture to the prepared pan and bake in a preheated oven, 350°F, for 25 minutes until risen and just firm to the touch. Leave to cool before covering with a sheet of non-stick baking parchment and a damp clean dish cloth. Leave until completely cold.

7 Turn the roulade out on to another piece of baking parchment dusted with confectioner's sugar and remove the lining paper.

8 Spread the cream over the roulade. Starting from a short end, roll the sponge away from you using the paper to guide you. Trim the ends of the roulade to make a neat finish and transfer to a serving plate. Leave to chill in the refrigerator until ready to serve. Dust with a little confectioners' sugar before serving, if wished.

Tiramisu

This is a traditional chocolate dessert from Italy, although at one time it was known as Zuppa Inglese *because it was a favorite with the English society living in Florence in the 1800's.*

Serves 6

INGREDIENTS

10¹/₂ oz dark chocolate
14 oz mascarpone cheese
²/₃ cup heavy cream, whipped until it
    just holds its shape

14 fl oz black coffee with
    1³/₄ oz superfine sugar, cooled
6 tbsp dark rum or brandy

36 lady's fingers,
    about 14 oz cocoa powder, to dust

1 Melt the chocolate in a bowl set over a saucepan of simmering water, stirring occasionally. Leave the chocolate to cool slightly, then stir it into the mascarpone and cream.

2 Mix the coffee and rum together in a bowl. Dip the lady's fingers into the mixture briefly so that they absorb the liquid but do not become soggy.

3 Place 3 lady's fingers on 3 serving plates.

4 Spoon a layer of the mascarpone and chocolate mixture over the lady's fingers.

5 Place 3 more lady's fingers on top of the mascarpone layer. Spread another layer of mascarpone and chocolate mixture and place 3 more lady's fingers on top.

6 Leave the tiramisu to chill in the refrigerator for at least 1 hour. Dust with a little cocoa powder just before serving.

COOK'S TIP

Tiramisu can also be served semi-frozen, like ice-cream. Freeze the tiramisu for 2 hours and serve immediately as it defrosts very quickly.

VARIATION

Try adding 1³/₄ oz toasted, chopped hazelnuts to the chocolate cream mixture in step 1, if you prefer.

Profiteroles with Banana Cream

*Chocolate profiteroles are a popular choice. In this recipe they are filled with
a delicious banana-flavored cream – the perfect combination!*

Serves 4–6

INGREDIENTS

CHOUX PASTRY:
2/3 cup water
1/4 cup butter
3/4 cup strong all-purpose flour, sifted
2 eggs

CHOCOLATE SAUCE:
3 1/2 oz dark chocolate, broken into pieces
2 tbsp water
4 tbsp confectioners' sugar
2 tbsp unsalted butter

FILLING:
1 1/4 cups heavy cream
1 banana
2 tbsp confectioners' sugar
2 tbsp banana-flavored liqueur

1 Lightly grease a baking sheet and sprinkle with a little water. To make the pastry, place the water in a pan. Cut the butter into small pieces and add to the pan. Heat gently until the butter melts, then bring to a rolling boil. Remove the pan from the heat and add the flour in one go, beating well until the mixture leaves the sides of the pan and forms a ball. Leave to cool slightly, then gradually beat in the eggs to form a smooth, glossy mixture.

Spoon the paste into a large pastry bag fitted with a 1/2 inch plain tip.

2 Pipe about 18 small balls of the paste on to the baking sheet, allowing enough room for them to expand during cooking. Bake in a preheated oven, 425°F, for 15-20 minutes until crisp and golden. Remove from the oven and make a small slit in each one for steam to escape. Cool on a wire rack.

3 To make the sauce, place all the ingredients in a heatproof bowl, set over a pan of simmering water and heat until combined to make a smooth sauce, stirring.

4 To make the filling, whip the cream until standing in soft peaks. Mash the banana with the sugar and liqueur. Fold into the cream. Place in a pastry bag fitted with a 1/2 inch plain tip and pipe into the profiteroles. Serve with the sauce poured over.

Chocolate Mousse

*This is a light and fluffy, but fruity-tasting mousse which
is delicious with a fresh fruit sauce.*

Serves 8

INGREDIENTS

3^1/$_2$ oz dark chocolate, melted
1^1/$_4$ cups unsweetened yogurt
^{2}/$_3$ cup quark
4 tbsp superfine sugar
1 tbsp orange juice
1 tbsp brandy

1^1/$_2$ tsp gelozone
9 tbsp cold water
2 large egg whites

coarsely grated dark and white
chocolate and orange zest, to
decorate

1 Put the melted chocolate,
unsweetened yogurt, quark,
superfine sugar, orange juice, and
brandy in a food processor and
blend for 30 seconds. Transfer the
mixture to a large bowl.

2 Sprinkle the gelozone over
the water and stir until
dissolved.

3 In a small saucepan, bring
the gelozone and water to
a boil for 2 minutes. Leave to cool
slightly, then stir into the

chocolate mixture.

4 Whisk the egg whites until
stiff peaks form and fold into
the chocolate mixture using a
metal spoon.

5 Line a 1^1/$_2$ pint loaf pan with
plastic wrap. Spoon the
mousse into the pan. Chill for
2 hours in the refrigerator until
set. Turn the mousse out on to a
plate, decorate and serve.

COOK'S TIP

*For a quick fruit sauce,
blend a can of mandarin segments
in unsweetened juice in a food
processor and press through a
strainer. Stir in 1 tbsp clear honey
and serve with the mousse.*

Champagne Mousse

A wonderful champagne-flavored mouse is served in chocolate sponge cups for an elegant dessert. Any dry sparkling wine made by the traditional method used for champagne can be used.

Serves 4

INGREDIENTS

SPONGE:
4 eggs
7 tbsp superfine sugar
2/3 cup self-rising flour
2 tbsp cocoa powder
2 tbsp butter, melted

MOUSSE:
1 envelope gelatin
3 tbsp water
1 1/4 cups champagne
1 1/4 cups heavy cream
2 egg whites
1/3 cup superfine sugar

TO DECORATE:
2 oz dark chocolate-flavored cake covering, melted
fresh strawberries

1 Line a 15 × 10 inch jelly-roll pan with greased baking parchment. Place the eggs and sugar in a bowl and whisk with electric beaters until the mixture is very thick and the whisk leaves a trail when lifted. If using a balloon whisk, stand the bowl over a pan of hot water whilst whisking. Sift the flour and cocoa together and fold into the egg mixture. Fold in the butter. Pour into the pan and bake in a preheated oven, 400°F, for 8 minutes or until springy to the touch. Cool for 5 minutes, then turn out on to a wire rack until cold. Line four 4 inch baking rings with baking parchment. Line the sides with 1 inch strips of cake and the base with circles.

2 To make the mousse, sprinkle the gelatin over the water and leave to go spongy. Place the bowl over a pan of hot water; stir until dissolved. Stir in the champagne.

3 Whip the cream until just holding its shape. Fold in the champagne mixture. Leave in a cool place until on the point of setting, stirring. Whisk the egg whites until standing in soft peaks, add the sugar and whisk until glossy. Fold into the setting mixture. Spoon into the sponge cases, allowing the mixture to go above the sponge. Chill for 2 hours. Pipe the cake covering in squiggles on a piece of parchment; leave to set. Decorate the mousses.

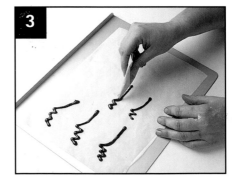

Chocolate Brandy Torte

A crumbly ginger chocolate base, topped with velvety smooth chocolate brandy cream makes this a blissful cake.

Serves 12

INGREDIENTS

BASE:
9 oz gingernut coolies
2³/₄ oz dark chocolate
generous ¹/₃ cup butter

FILLING:
8 oz dark chocolate
9 oz mascarpone cheese
2 eggs, separated
3 tbsp brandy
1¹/₄ cups heavy cream
4 tbsp superfine sugar

TO DECORATE:
scant ¹/₂ cup heavy cream
chocolate coffee beans

1 Crush the cookies in a bag with a rolling pin or in a food processor. Melt the chocolate and butter together and pour over the cookies. Mix well, then use to line the base and sides of a 9 inch loose-bottomed fluted flan pan or springform pan. Leave to chill whilst preparing the filling.

2 To make the filling, melt the dark chocolate in a pan, remove from the heat and beat in the mascarpone cheese, egg yolks, and brandy.

3 Lightly whip the cream until just holding its shape and fold in the chocolate mixture.

4 Whisk the egg whites in a grease-free bowl until standing in soft peaks. Add the superfine sugar a little at a time and whisk until thick and glossy. Fold into the chocolate mixture, in 2 batches, until just mixed.

5 Spoon the mixture into the prepared base and chill for at least 2 hours. Carefully transfer to a serving plate. To decorate, whip the cream and pipe on to the cheesecake and add the chocolate coffee beans.

VARIATION

If chocolate coffee beans are unavailable, use chocolate-coated raisins to decorate.

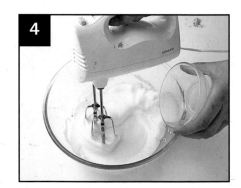

Chocolate Rum Pots

*Wickedly rich little pots, flavored with a hint
of dark rum, for pure indulgence!*

Serves 6

INGREDIENTS

8 oz dark chocolate
4 eggs, separated
1/3 cup superfine sugar

4 tbsp dark rum
4 tbsp heavy cream

TO DECORATE:
a little whipped cream
chocolate shapes (see page 242)

1 Melt the chocolate and leave to cool slightly.

2 Whisk the egg yolks with the superfine sugar in a bowl until very pale and fluffy; this will take about 5 minutes with electric beaters, a little longer with a balloon whisk.

3 Drizzle the chocolate into the mixture and fold in together with the rum and the heavy cream.

4 Whisk the egg whites in a grease-free bowl until standing in soft peaks. Fold the egg whites into the chocolate mixture in 2 batches. Divide the mixture between 6 ramekins, or other individual dishes, and leave to chill for at least 2 hours.

5 To serve, decorate with a little whipped cream and small chocolate shapes.

VARIATION

These delicious little pots can be flavored with brandy instead of rum, if preferred.

COOK'S TIP

Make sure you use a perfectly clean and grease-free bowl for whisking the egg whites. They will not aerate if any grease is present as the smallest amount breaks down the bubbles in the whites, preventing them from trapping and holding air.

Breads & Savories

Freshly baked bread has never been easier to make, especially with the quick-rising yeasts available nowadays. In this chapter ¹/₄ oz envelopes of easy-blend dried yeast have been used as it is easy to obtain, simple to use, and gives good results. If you want to use fresh yeast, replace one envelope of quick-rising yeast with 1 oz of fresh yeast. Blend the fresh yeast into the warm liquid and add 1 teaspoon of sugar. Add to the flour and continue as usual.

Always choose a white or brown bread flour for the bread recipes using yeast, it contains a high proportion of gluten, the protein which gives the dough its elasticity. Always knead the dough thoroughly – this can be done in an electric mixer with the dough hook attachment for about 5-8 minutes, but kneading by hand is most enjoyable and allows the cook the pleasure of relieving their aggression and stress upon the dough!

This chapter also includes a selection of savories to savor, including a tasty selection of pies, pastries, and flans to create a whole medley of delicious dishes that can be used as part of a main meal.

Banana & Date Loaf

*This tea bread is excellent for afternoon tea or coffee time
with its moist texture and more-ish flavor.*

Serves 8-10

INGREDIENTS

2 cups self-rising
  flour
$1/3$ cup butter, cut into small pieces
$1/3$ cup superfine sugar

125 g/$4^1/_2$ oz pitted dates, chopped
2 bananas, mashed roughly
2 eggs, beaten lightly
2 tbsp honey

1 Grease a 2 lb loaf pan and line the base with baking parchment.

2 Sift the flour into a mixing bowl.

3 Rub the butter into the flour with your fingertips until the mixture resembles fine bread crumbs.

4 Stir the sugar, chopped dates, bananas, beaten eggs, and honey into the dry ingredients. Mix together to form a soft dropping consistency.

5 Spoon the mixture into the prepared loaf pan and level the surface with the back of a knife.

6 Bake in a preheated oven, 325°F, for about 1 hour or until golden and a fine metal skewer inserted into the center comes out clean.

7 Leave the loaf to cool in the pan before turning out and transferring to a wire rack.

8 Serve the loaf warm or cold, cut into thick slices.

COOK'S TIP

This tea bread will keep for several days if stored in an airtight container and kept in a cool, dry place.

Date & Honey Loaf

This bread is full of good things – chopped dates, sesame seeds, and honey.
Toast thick slices and spread with soft cheese for a light snack.

Makes 1 loaf

INGREDIENTS

1¼ cups white bread flour
¼ cup bread brown bread flour

½ tsp salt
1 envelope quick-rising dried yeast
¾ cup tepid water
3 tbsp sunflower oil

3 tbsp honey
2¾ oz dates, chopped
2 tbsp sesame seeds

1 Grease a 2 lb loaf pan. Sift the flours into a large mixing bowl, stir in the salt and dried yeast.

2 Pour in the tepid water, oil and honey. Mix everything together to form a dough.

3 Place the dough on a lightly floured surface and knead for about 5 minutes until smooth.

4 Place the dough in a greased bowl, cover, and leave to rise in a warm place for about 1 hour or until doubled in size.

5 Knead in the dates and sesame seeds. Shape the dough and place in the pan.

6 Cover and leave in a warm place for a further 30 minutes or until springy to the touch.

7 Bake in a preheated oven, 425°F, for 30 minutes or until a hollow sound is heard when the base of the loaf is tapped.

8 Transfer the loaf to a wire rack and leave to cool. Serve cut into thick slices.

COOK'S TIP

If you cannot find a warm place, sit a bowl with the dough in it over a saucepan of warm water and cover.

VARIATION

Replace the sesame seeds with sunflower seeds for a slightly different texture, if you prefer.

Cinnamon & Currant Loaf

This spicy, fruit tea bread is quick and easy to make. Serve it buttered and with a drizzle of honey for an afternoon snack.

Makes a 2 lb loaf

INGREDIENTS

3 cups all-purpose flour
pinch of salt
1 tbsp baking powder
1 tbsp ground cinnamon

$^2/_3$ cup butter, cut into small pieces
$^3/_4$ cup soft brown sugar
$^3/_4$ cup currants

finely grated rind of 1 orange
5-6 tbsp orange juice
6 tbsp milk
2 eggs, beaten lightly

1 Grease a 2 lb loaf pan and line the base smoothly with baking parchment.

2 Sift the flour, salt, baking powder, and ground cinnamon into a bowl. Then rub in the pieces of butter with your fingers, until the mixture resembles coarse bread crumbs.

3 Stir in the sugar, currants, and orange rind. Beat the orange juice, milk, and eggs together and add to the dry ingredients. Mix well together.

4 Spoon the mixture into the prepared pan. Make a slight dip in the middle of the mixture to help it rise evenly.

5 Bake in a preheated oven, 350°F, for about 1-1 hour 10 minutes, or until a fine metal skewer inserted into the center of the loaf comes out clean.

6 Leave the loaf to cool before turning out of the pan. Transfer to a wire rack and leave to cool completely before slicing.

COOK'S TIP

Once you have added the liquid to the dry ingredients, work as quickly as possible because the baking powder is activated by the liquid.

Orange, Banana, & Cranberry Loaf

The addition of chopped nuts, mixed peel, fresh orange juice,
and dried cranberries makes this a rich, moist tea bread.

Serves 8-10

INGREDIENTS

1¹/₂ cups self-rising flour
¹/₂ tsp baking powder
1 cup soft brown sugar
2 bananas, mashed

1³/₄ oz chopped mixed peel
1 oz chopped mixed nuts
1³/₄ oz dried cranberries
5-6 tbsp orange juice
2 eggs, beaten

²/₃ cup sunflower oil
2³/₄ oz confectioners' sugar, sifted
grated rind of 1 orange

1 Grease a 2 lb loaf pan and line the base with baking parchment.

2 Sift the flour and baking powder into a mixing bowl. Then stir in the sugar, bananas, chopped mixed peel, nuts, and cranberries.

3 Stir the orange juice, eggs, and oil together until well combined. Add the mixture to the dry ingredients and mix until well blended. Pour the mixture into the prepared pan.

4 Bake in a preheated oven, 350°F, for about 1 hour until firm to the touch or until a fine skewer inserted into the center of the loaf comes out clean.

5 Turn out the loaf and leave it to cool on a wire rack.

6 Mix the confectioners' sugar with a little water and drizzle the frosting over the loaf. Sprinkle the orange rind over the top. Leave the frosting to set before serving the loaf in slices.

COOK'S TIP

This tea bread will keep for a couple of days. Wrap it carefully and store in a cool, dry place.

Crown Loaf

This is a rich sweet bread combining alcohol, nuts, and fruit in a decorative wreath shape. It is ideal for serving at Christmas-time. You can omit the frosting and glaze with 2 tbsp honey, if preferred.

Makes 1 loaf

INGREDIENTS

2 cups white bread flour
$^1/_2$ tsp salt
1 envelope quick-rising dried yeast
6 tsp butter, cut into small pieces
$^1/_2$ cup tepid milk
1 egg, beaten

FILLING:
$1^3/_4$ oz butter, softened
3 tbsp soft brown sugar
1 oz chopped hazelnuts

1 oz candied ginger, chopped
$1^3/_4$ oz candied peel
1 tbsp rum or brandy
$^2/_3$ cup confectioners' sugar
2 tbsp lemon juice

1 Grease a baking sheet. Sift the flour and salt into a bowl. Stir in the yeast. Rub in the butter with your fingers. Add the milk and egg and mix together to form a dough.

2 Place the dough in a greased bowl, cover and leave in a warm place for 40 minutes until doubled in size. Knead the dough lightly for 1 minute to punch down. Roll out to a rectangle 12 x 9 inches.

3 To make the filling, cream together the butter and sugar until light and fluffy. Stir in the hazelnuts, ginger, candied peel, and rum or brandy. Spread the filling over the dough, leaving a 1 inch border.

4 Roll up the dough, starting from the long edge, to form a sausage shape. Cut into slices at 2 inch intervals and lay on the baking sheet. Cover and leave to rise for 30 minutes.

5 Bake in a preheated oven, 325°F, for 20-30 minutes or until golden. Meanwhile, mix the confectioners' sugar with enough lemon juice to form a thin frosting.

6 Leave the loaf to cool slightly before drizzling the whole circle with frosting. Allow the frosting to set slightly before serving the loaf.

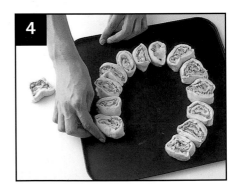

Pumpkin Loaf

The pumpkin purée in this loaf makes it beautifully moist.
It is delicious eaten at any time of the day.

Serves 6-8

INGREDIENTS

1 lb pumpkin flesh
$^1\!/_2$ cup butter, softened
$^3\!/_4$ cup superfine sugar

2 eggs, beaten
2 cups all-purpose flour, sifted
$1^1\!/_2$ tsp baking powder

$^1\!/_2$ tsp salt
1 tsp ground allspice
1 oz pumpkin seeds

1 Grease a 2 lb loaf pan with oil.

2 Chop the pumpkin into large pieces and wrap in buttered foil. Cook in a preheated oven, 400°F, for 30-40 minutes until they are tender.

3 Leave the pumpkin to cool completely before mashing well to make a thick purée.

4 In a bowl, cream the butter and sugar together until light and fluffy. Add the eggs a little at a time.

5 Stir in the pumpkin purée. Fold in the flour, baking powder, salt and allspice.

6 Fold the pumpkin seeds gently through the mixture. Spoon the mixture into the loaf pan.

7 Bake in a preheated oven, 325°F, for about $1^1\!/_4$-$1^1\!/_2$ hours or until a skewer inserted into the center of the loaf comes out clean.

8 Leave the loaf to cool and serve buttered, if wished.

COOK'S TIP

To ensure that the pumpkin purée is dry, place it in a saucepan over a medium heat for a few minutes, stirring frequently, until it is thick.

Mango Twist Bread

This is a sweet bread which has puréed mango mixed into the dough,
resulting in a moist loaf with an exotic flavor.

Makes 1 loaf

INGREDIENTS

4 cups white bread flour
1 tsp salt
1 envelope quick-rising dried yeast
1 tsp ground ginger
3 tbsp soft brown sugar
9 tsp butter, cut into small pieces

1 small mango, peeled, cored, and
    puréed
generous 1 cup tepid water
2 tbsp runny honey
2/3 cup golden raisins
1 egg, beaten

confectioners' sugar,
    for dusting

1 Grease a baking sheet. sift the flour and salt into a large mixing bowl, stir in the dried yeast, ground ginger and brown sugar. Rub in the butter with your fingers.

2 Stir in the mango purée, water and honey and mix together to form a dough.

3 Place the dough on a lightly floured surface and knead for about 5 minutes until smooth (alternatively, use an electric mixer with a dough hook). Place the dough in a greased bowl, cover and leave to rise in a warm place for about 1 hour until it has doubled in size.

4 Knead in the golden raisins and shape the dough into 2 sausage shapes, each 10 inches long. Carefully twist the 2 pieces together and pinch the ends to seal. Place the dough on the baking sheet, cover and leave in a warm place for a further 40 minutes.

5 Brush the loaf with the egg and bake in a preheated oven, 425°F, for 30 minutes until golden brown. Leave to cool on a wire rack. Dust with confectioners' sugar before serving.

COOK'S TIP

You can tell when the bread is
cooked as it will sound hollow
when tapped on the bottom.

Chocolate Bread

*For the chocoholics among us, this bread is great
fun to make and even better to eat.*

Makes 1 loaf

INGREDIENTS

4 cups white bread flour
1/4 cup cocoa powder

1 tsp salt
1 envelope quick-rising dried yeast
6 tsp soft brown sugar

1 tbsp oil
1 1/3 cups tepid water

1 Lightly grease a 2 lb loaf pan.

2 Sift the flour and cocoa powder into a large mixing bowl.

3 Stir in the salt, dried yeast, and brown sugar.

4 Pour in the oil along with the tepid water and mix the ingredients together to make a dough.

5 Place the dough on a lightly floured surface and knead for 5 minutes.

6 Place the dough in a greased bowl, cover, and leave to rise in a warm place for about 1 hour or until the dough has doubled in size.

7 Punch down the dough and shape it into a loaf. Place the dough in the prepared pan, cover, and leave to rise in a wam place for a further 30 minutes.

8 Bake in a preheated oven, 400°F, for 25-30 minutes, or until a hollow sound is heard when the base of the bread is tapped.

9 Transfer the bread to a wire rack and leave to cool. Cut into slices to serve.

COOK'S TIP

This bread can be sliced and spread with butter or it can be lightly toasted.

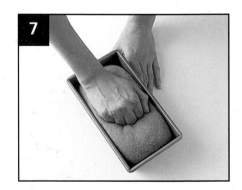

Thyme Crescents

These savory crescent snacks are very similar to croissants and are perfect for a quick and tasty bite to eat. They can also be shaped into twists, if preferred.

Makes 8

INGREDIENTS

9 oz fresh ready-made puff pastry
$1/3$ cup butter, softened

1 garlic clove, minced
1 tsp lemon juice

1 tsp dried thyme
salt and pepper

1 Lightly grease a baking sheet.

2 On a lightly floured surface, roll out the pastry to form a 10 inch round and cut into 8 wedges.

3 In a small bowl, mix the softened butter, garlic clove, lemon juice, and dried thyme together until soft. Season with salt and pepper to taste.

4 Spread a little of the butter and thyme mixture on to each wedge of pastry, dividing it equally between them.

5 Carefully roll up each wedge, starting from the wide end.

6 Arrange the crescents on the prepared baking sheet and chill for 30 minutes.

7 Dampen the baking sheet with cold water. This will create a steamy atmosphere in the oven while the crescents are baking and help the pastries to rise.

8 Bake in a preheated oven, 400°F, for 10-15 minutes until the crescents are well risen and golden.

COOK'S TIP

Dried herbs have a stronger flavor than fresh ones, which makes them perfect for these pastries. The crescents can be made with other dried herbs of your choice, such as rosemary and sage, or mixed herbs.

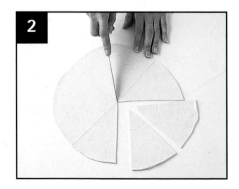

Chili Corn Bread

*This Mexican-style corn bread makes a great accompaniment
to chili or it can be eaten on its own as a tasty snack.*

Makes 12 bars

INGREDIENTS

1 cup all-purpose flour
4$^1/_2$ oz polenta
1 tbsp baking powder
$^1/_2$ tsp salt

1 green chili, seeded and
  chopped finely
5 scallions, chopped finely
2 eggs

generous $^1/_2$ cup soured cream
$^1/_2$ cup sunflower oil

1 Grease a 8 inch square cake pan and line the base with baking parchment.

2 In a large bowl, mix the flour, polenta, baking powder, and salt together.

3 Add the finely chopped green chili and the spring scallions to the dry ingredients and mix well.

4 In a mixing pitcher, beat the eggs together with the soured cream, and sunflower oil. Pour the mixture into the bowl of dry ingredients. Mix everything together quickly and thoroughly.

5 Pour the mixture into the prepared cake pan.

6 Bake in a preheated oven, 400°F, for 20-25 minutes or until the loaf has risen and is lightly browned.

7 Leave the bread to cool slightly before turning out of the pan. Cut into bars or squares to serve.

VARIATION

*Add 4$^1/_2$ oz of corn kernels to the
mixture in step 3,
if you prefer.*

Cheese & Potato Bread

This lovely cheesy bread is ideal for a quick savory snack.
The mashed potato gives it a lovely moist texture.

Makes 1 loaf

INGREDIENTS

2 cups all-purpose flour
1 tsp salt

$^1/_2$ tsp mustard powder
2 tsp baking powder
$4^1/_2$ oz Red Leicester cheese, grated
6 oz potatoes, cooked and mashed

$^3/_4$ cup water
1 tbsp oil

1 Lightly grease a baking sheet.

2 Sift the flour, salt, mustard powder, and baking powder into a mixing bowl.

3 Reserve 2 tbsp of the grated cheese and stir the rest into the bowl with the cooked and mashed potatoes.

4 Pour in the water and the oil, and stir all the ingredients together (the mixture will be wet at this stage). Mix them all to make a soft dough.

5 Turn out the dough on to a floured surface and shape it into a 8 inch round.

6 Place the round on the baking sheet and mark it into 4 portions with a knife, without cutting through. Sprinkle with the reserved cheese.

7 Bake in a preheated oven, 425°F, for 25-30 minutes.

8 Transfer the bread to a wire rack and leave to cool. Serve the bread as fresh as possible.

COOK'S TIP

You can use instant potato mix for this bread, if wished.

VARIATION

Add $1^3/_4$ oz chopped ham to the mixture in step 3, if you prefer.

Sun-Dried Tomato Rolls

These white rolls have the addition of finely chopped sun-dried tomatoes.
The tomatoes are sold in jars and are readily available at most supermarkets.

Makes 8

INGREDIENTS

2 cups white bread flour
$^1/_2$ tsp salt
1 envelope quick-rising dried yeast

$^1/_3$ cup butter, melted and cooled
  slightly
3 tbsp milk, warmed
2 eggs, beaten

1$^3/_4$ oz sun-dried tomatoes, well
  drained and chopped finely
milk, for brushing

1 Lightly grease a baking sheet.

2 Sift the flour and salt into a large mixing bowl. Stir in the yeast, then pour in the butter, milk, and eggs. Mix together to form a dough.

3 Turn the dough on to a lightly floured surface and knead for about 5 minutes (alternatively, use an electric mixer with a dough hook).

4 Place the dough in a greased bowl, cover and leave to rise

in a warm place for 1-1$^1/_2$ hours until the dough has doubled in size. Punch down the dough by kneading it for a few minutes.

5 Knead the sun-dried tomatoes into the dough, sprinkling the work counter with extra flour as the tomatoes are quite oily.

6 Divide the dough into 8 balls and place them on to the baking sheet. Cover and leave to rise for about 30 minutes until the rolls have doubled in size.

7 Brush the rolls with milk and bake in a preheated oven, 450°F, for 10-15 minutes until the rolls are golden brown.

8 Transfer the rolls to a wire rack and leave to cool slightly before serving.

COOK'S TIP

The quick-rising dried yeast used in this recipe is widely available in most supermarkets.

Savory Curried Crackers

When making these crackers, try different types of curry powder strengths until you find the one that suits your own tastes.

Makes 40

INGREDIENTS

$^3/_4$ cup all-purpose flour
1 tsp salt
2 tsp curry powder

$3^1/_2$ oz mellow hard cheese, grated
$3^1/_2$ oz Parmesan cheese, grated

$^1/_3$ cup butter, softened

1 Lightly grease about 4 baking sheets.

2 Sift the all-purpose flour and salt into a mixing bowl.

3 Stir in the curry powder and the grated mellow hard and Parmesan cheeses. Rub in the softened butter with your fingers until the mixture comes together to form a soft dough.

4 On a lightly floured surface, roll out the dough thinly to form a rectangle.

5 Using a 2 inch cookie cutter, cut out 40 round crackers.

6 Arrange the crackers on the baking sheets.

7 Bake in a preheated oven, 350°F, for 10-15 minutes.

8 Leave the crackers to cool slightly on the baking sheets. Transfer the crackers to a wire rack until completely cold and crisp, then serve.

COOK'S TIP

These crackers can be stored for several days in an airtight pan or plastic container.

Cheese & Onion Pies

These crisp pies are filled with a tasty onion, garlic, and parsley mixture, making them ideal for lunch boxes.

Makes 4

INGREDIENTS

'3 tbsp vegetable oil
4 onions, peeled and sliced finely
4 garlic cloves, minced
4 tbsp finely chopped fresh
   parsley
2³/₄ oz sharp cheese, grated
salt and pepper

PASTRY:
1¹/₂ cups all-purpose flour
¹/₂ tsp salt

¹/₃ cup butter, cut into small pieces
3-4 tbsp water

1 Heat the oil in a skillet. Add the onions and garlic and fry for 10-15 minutes or until the onions are soft. Remove the skillet from the heat and stir in the parsley and cheese and season.

2 To make the pastry, sift the flour and salt into a mixing bowl and rub in the butter with your fingertips until the mixture resembles bread crumbs. Stir in the water and mix to a dough.

3 On a lightly floured surface, roll out the dough and divide it into 8 portions.

4 Roll out each portion to a 4 inch round and use half of the rounds to line 4 individual tart pans.

5 Fill each round with a quarter of the onion mixture. Cover with the remaining 4 pastry rounds. Make a slit in the top of each tart with the point of a knife and seal the edges with the back of a teaspoon.

6 Bake in a preheated oven, 425°F, for 20 minutes. Serve hot or cold.

COOK'S TIP

You can prepare the onion filling in advance and store it in the refrigerator until required.

Puff Potato Pie

This pie with its rich filling is a great alternative to serving potatoes as a side dish with any meal. Alternatively, serve with salad for a light lunch.

Serves 6

INGREDIENTS

1 lb 9 oz potatoes, peeled and sliced thinly
2 scallions, chopped finely

1 red onion, chopped finely
2/3 cup heavy cream

1 lb fresh ready-made puff pastry
2 eggs, beaten
salt and pepper

1 Lightly grease a baking sheet. Bring a saucepan of water to a boil, add the sliced potatoes, bring back to a boil, and then simmer for a few minutes. Drain the potato slices and leave to cool. Dry off any excess moisture with paper towels.

2 In a bowl, mix together the spring scallions, red onion, and the cooled potato slices. Stir in 2 tbsp of the cream and plenty of seasoning.

3 Divide the pastry in half and roll out one piece to a 9 inch round. Roll the remaining pastry to a 10 inch round.

4 Place the smaller circle on to the baking sheet and top with the potato mixture, leaving a 1 inch border. Brush this border with a little of the beaten egg.

5 Top with the larger circle of pastry, seal well, and crimp the edges of the pastry. Cut a steam vent in the middle of the pastry and mark with a pattern. Brush with the beaten egg and bake in a preheated oven, 400°F, for 30 minutes.

6 Mix the remaining beaten egg with the rest of the cream and pour into the pie through the steam vent. Return to the oven for 15 minutes, then leave to cool for 30 minutes. Serve warm or cold.

COOK'S TIP

The filling maybe prepared up to 4 hours in advance.

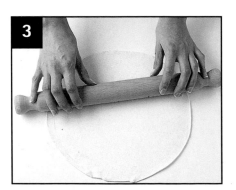

Celery & Onion Pies

These savory celery and onion pies are quite irresistible,
so it is probably a good idea to bake a double batch!

Makes 1 loaf

INGREDIENTS

PASTRY:
1 cup all-purpose flour
$^1/_2$ tsp salt
6 tsp butter, cut into small pieces

1 oz sharp cheese, grated
3-4 tbsp water

FILLING:
10 tsp butter
4$^1/_2$ oz celery, chopped finely
2 garlic cloves, minced

1 small onion, chopped finely
1 tbsp all-purpose flour
$^1/_4$ cup milk
salt
pinch of cayenne pepper

1 To make the filling, melt the butter in a skillet. Add the celery, garlic, and onion and fry gently for about 5 minutes or until soft.

2 Reduce the heat and stir in the flour, then the milk. Bring back to a simmer, then heat gently until the mixture is thick, stirring frequently.

3 Season with salt and cayenne pepper. Leave to cool.

4 To make the pastry, sift the flour and salt into a mixing bowl and rub in the butter with your fingers. Stir the cheese into the mixture together with the cold water and mix to form a dough.

5 Roll out three quarters of the dough on to a lightly floured surface. Using a 2$^1/_2$ inch cookie cutter, cut out 12 rounds. Line a patty pan with the rounds.

6 Divide the filling between the pastry rounds. Roll out the remaining dough and, using a 2 inch cutter, cut out 12 circles. Place the smaller circles on top of the pie filling and seal well. Make a slit in each pie and leave to chill for 30 minutes.

7 Bake in a preheated oven, 425°F, for 15-20 minutes. Leave to cool in the pan for about 10 minutes before turning out. Serve warm.

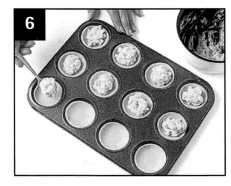

Red Onion Tart Tatin

*Ready-made puff pastry works extremely well in this recipe
and means you create a quick savory tart in very little time.*

Serves 4

INGREDIENTS

10 tsp butter
6 tsp sugar
1 lb red onions, peeled and quartered

3 tbsp red wine vinegar
2 tbsp fresh thyme leaves
8 oz fresh ready-made puff pastry

salt and pepper

1 Place the butter and sugar in a 9 inch ovenproof skillet and cook over a medium heat until melted.

2 Add the red onion quarters and sweat them over a low heat for 10-15 minutes until golden, stirring occasionally.

3 Add the red wine vinegar and thyme leaves to the pan. Season with salt and pepper to taste, then simmer over a medium heat until the liquid has reduced and the red onion pieces are coated in the buttery sauce.

4 On a lightly floured surface, roll out the pastry to a circle slightly larger than the skillet.

5 Place the pastry over the onion mixture and press down, tucking in the edges to seal the pastry.

6 Bake in a preheated oven, 350°F, for 20-25 minutes. Leave the tart to stand for 10 minutes.

7 To turn out, place a serving plate over the skillet and carefully invert them both so that the pastry becomes the base of the tart. Serve the tart warm.

VARIATION

Replace the red onions with shallots, leaving them whole, if you prefer.

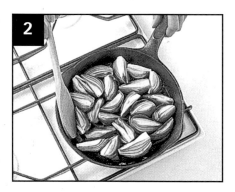

Onion Tart

*This crisp pie shell is filled with onions and
cheese and baked until it melts in the mouth.*

Serves 6

INGREDIENTS

9 oz fresh ready-made shortcrust
  pastry
8 tsp butter
2³/₄ oz bacon, chopped

1lb 9 oz onions, peeled and sliced
  thinly
2 eggs, beaten
1³/₄ oz Parmesan cheese, grated

1 tsp dried sage
salt and pepper

1 Roll out the pastry on a
lightly floured surface and
line a 9¹/₂ inch loose-bottomed
flan pan.

2 Prick the base of the pastry
with a fork and leave to chill
for 30 minutes.

3 Heat the butter in a saucepan,
add the chopped bacon and
sliced onions and sweat them over
a low heat for about 25 minutes
until tender. If the onion slices
start to brown, add 1 tbsp water to
the saucepan.

4 Add the beaten eggs to the
onion mixture and stir in the
cheese, sage, and salt and pepper
to taste.

5 Spoon the onion mixture
into the prepared pie shell.

6 Bake in a preheated oven,
350°F, for 20-30 minutes or
until the tart has just set.

7 Leave to cool slightly in the
pan, then serve the tart warm
or cold.

VARIATION

*For a vegetarian version of this tart,
replace the bacon with the same
amount of chopped mushrooms.*

Fresh Tomato Tarts

*These tomato-flavored tarts should be eaten as fresh as possible
to enjoy the flaky and crisp buttery puff pastry.*

Serves 6

INGREDIENTS

9 oz fresh ready-made puff pastry
1 egg, beaten

2 tbsp pesto
6 plum tomatoes, sliced
salt and pepper

fresh thyme leaves, to garnish
(optional)

1 On a lightly floured surface, roll out the pastry to a area measuring 12 x 10 inches.

2 Cut the rectangle in half and divide each half into 3 pieces to make 6 even-sized rectangles. Leave to chill for 20 minutes.

3 Lightly score the edges of the pastry rectangles and brush with the beaten egg.

4 Spread the pesto over the rectangles, dividing it equally between them, leaving a 1 inch border on each one.

5 Arrange the tomato slices along the center of each rectangle on top of the pesto.

6 Season well with salt and pepper to taste and lightly sprinkle with fresh thyme leaves, if using.

7 Bake in a preheated oven, 400°F, for 15-20 minutes until well risen and golden brown.

8 Transfer the tomato tarts to warm serving plates straight from the oven and serve while they are still very hot.

VARIATION

Instead of individual tarts, roll the pastry out to form 1 large rectangle. Spoon over the pesto and arrange the tomatoes over the top.

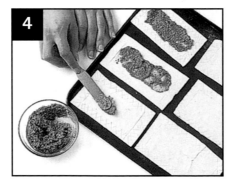

Asparagus & Goat's Cheese Tart

Fresh asparagus is now readily available all year round,
so you can make this tasty supper dish at any time.

Serves 6

INGREDIENTS

9 oz fresh ready-made shortcrust
   pastry
9 oz asparagus
1 tbsp vegetable oil

1 red onion, chopped finely
7 oz goat's cheese
1 oz hazelnuts, chopped

2 eggs, beaten
4 tbsp light cream
salt and pepper

1 On a lightly floured surface, roll out the pastry and line a 9½ inch loose-bottomed flan pan. Prick the base of the pastry with a fork and leave to chill for 30 minutes.

2 Line the pie shell with foil and baking beans and bake in a preheated oven, 375°F, for about 15 minutes.

3 Remove the foil and baking beans and cook for a further 15 minutes.

4 Cook the asparagus in boiling water for 2-3 minutes, drain and cut into bite-size pieces.

5 Heat the oil in a small skillet and fry the onion until soft and lightly golden. Spoon the asparagus, onion, and hazelnuts into the prepared pie shell.

6 Beat together the cheese, eggs, and cream until smooth, or process in a blender until smooth. Season well with salt and pepper, then pour the mixture over the asparagus, onion, and hazelnuts.

7 Bake in the oven for 15-20 minutes or until the cheese filling is just set. Serve warm or cold.

VARIATION

Omit the hazelnuts and sprinkle
Parmesan cheese over the top of the
tart just before cooking in the
oven, if you prefer.

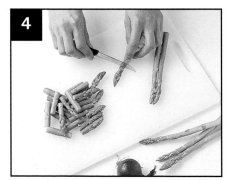

Provençal Tart

This tart is full of color and flavor from the zucchini and red and green bell peppers. It makes a great change from a quiche Lorraine.

Serves 6-8

INGREDIENTS

9 oz ready-made fresh puff pastry
3 tbsp olive oil
2 red bell peppers, seeded and diced
2 green bell peppers, seeded

and diced
²/₃ cup heavy cream
1 egg
2 zucchini, sliced

salt and pepper

1 Roll out the pastry on a lightly floured surface and line a 8 inch loose-bottomed flan pan. Leave to chill in the refrigerator for 20 minutes.

2 Meanwhile, heat 2 tbsp of the olive oil in a pan and fry the bell peppers for about 8 minutes until softened, stirring frequently.

3 Whisk the heavy cream and egg together in a bowl and season to taste with salt and pepper. Stir in the cooked bell peppers.

4 Heat the remaining oil in a pan and fry the zucchini slices for 4-5 minutes until lightly browned.

5 Pour the egg and bell pepper mixture into the pie shell.

6 Arrange the zucchini slices around the edge of the tart.

7 Bake in a preheated oven, 350°F, for 35-40 minutes or until just set and golden brown.

COOK'S TIP

This recipe could be used to make 6 individual tarts – use 6 x 4 inch pans and bake them for 20 minutes.

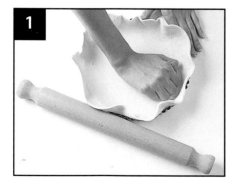

Ham & Cheese Lattice Pies

These pretty lattice pies are equally delicious served hot or cold.
They make a good picnic food served with salad.

Makes 6

INGREDIENTS

9 oz fresh ready-made puff pastry
1³/₄ oz ham, finely chopped

4¹/₂ oz full fat soft cheese
2 tbsp chopped fresh chives
1 egg, beaten

2 tbsp freshly grated Parmesan
 cheese
pepper

1 Roll out the pastry thinly on to a lightly floured work counter. Cut out 12 rectangles measuring 6 x 2 inches.

2 Place the rectangles on to greased baking sheets and leave to chill in the refrigerator for 30 minutes.

3 Meanwhile, combine the ham, cheese, and chives in a small bowl. Season with pepper to taste.

4 Spread the ham and cheese mixture along the center of 6 of the rectangles, leaving a

1 inch border around each one. Brush the border with the beaten egg.

5 To make the lattice pattern, fold the remaining rectangles lengthways. Leaving a 1 inch border, cut vertical lines across one edge of the rectangles.

6 Unfold the rectangles and place them over the rectangles topped with the ham and cheese mixture set on the baking sheets. Seal the pastry edges well and lightly sprinkle with the Parmesan cheese.

7 Bake in a preheated oven, 350°F, for 15-20 minutes. Serve hot or cold.

COOK'S TIP

These pies can be made in advance, frozen uncooked and baked fresh when required.

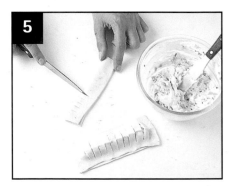

Curry Pasties

*These pasties, which are suitable for vegans, are a delicious combination
of vegetables and spices. They can be eaten either hot or cold.*

Makes 1 loaf

INGREDIENTS

1³/4 cups all-purpose whole-wheat
  flour
¹/3 cup vegan margarine, cut into
  small pieces
4 tbsp water
2 tbsp oil

8 oz diced root vegetables (potatoes,
  carrots, and parsnips)
1 small onion, chopped
2 garlic cloves, chopped finely
¹/2 tsp curry powder
¹/2 tsp ground turmeric

¹/2 tsp ground cumin
¹/2 tsp whole-grain mustard
5 tbsp vegetable stock
soya milk, to glaze

1 Place the flour in a mixing
bowl and rub in the vegan
margarine with your fingertips
until the mixture resembles bread
crumbs. Stir in the water and
bring together to form a soft
dough. Wrap and leave to chill in
the refrigerator for 30 minutes.

2 To make the filling, heat the
oil in a large saucepan. Add
the diced root vegetables, chopped
onion, and garlic. Fry for 2
minutes, then stir in all of the
spices, turning the vegetables to

coat them with the spices. Fry the
vegetables for a further 1 minute.

3 Add the stock to the pan and
bring to a boil. Cover and
simmer for about 20 minutes,
stirring occasionally, until the
vegetables are tender and the liquid
has been absorbed. Leave to cool.

4 Divide the pastry into 4
portions. Roll each portion
into a 6 inch round. Place the
filling on one half of each round.

5 Brush the edges of each
round with soya milk, then
fold over and press the edges
together to seal. Place on a baking
sheet. Bake in a preheated oven,
400°F, for 25-30 minutes until the
pastry is golden brown.

COOK'S TIP

*The vegetable filling can be
made in advance and stored in the
refrigerator until required.*

Pissaladière

This is a variation of the classic Italian pizza but is made with ready-made puff pastry. It is perfect for outdoor eating.

Serves 8

INGREDIENTS

4 tbsp olive oil
1 lb 9 oz red onions, sliced thinly
2 garlic cloves, minced
2 tsp superfine sugar

2 tbsp red wine vinegar
12 oz fresh ready-made puff pastry
salt and pepper

TOPPING:
$1^3/4$ oz cans anchovy fillets
12 green pitted olives
1 tsp dried marjoram

1 Lightly grease a jelly-roll pan. Heat the olive oil in a large saucepan. Add the onions and garlic and cook over a low heat for about 30 minutes, stirring occasionally.

2 Add the sugar and red wine vinegar to the pan and season with plenty of salt and pepper.

3 On a lightly floured surface, roll out the pastry to a rectangle about 13 x 9 inches. Place the pastry rectangle on to the prepared pan, pushing the pastry well into the corners of the pan.

4 Spread the onion mixture over the pastry.

5 Arrange the anchovy fillets and green olives on top, then sprinkle with the marjoram.

6 Bake in a preheated oven, 425°F, for about 20-25 minutes until the pissaladière is lightly golden. Serve very hot, straight from the oven.

VARIATION

Cut the pissaladière into squares or triangles for easy finger food at a party or grill.

Mini Cheese & Onion Tarts

*Serve these delicious little savory tarts as finger food
at buffets or drinks parties.*

Serves 12

INGREDIENTS

PASTRY:
1 cup all-purpose flour
$^{1}/_{4}$ tsp salt
$^{1}/_{3}$ cup butter, cut into small pieces
1-2 tbsp water

FILLING:
1 egg, beaten

generous $^{1}/_{3}$ cup light cream
$1^{3}/_{4}$ oz Red Leicester cheese, grated

3 scallions, chopped finely
salt
cayenne pepper

1 To make the pastry, sift the flour and salt into a mixing bowl. Rub in the butter with your fingers until the mixture resembles bread crumbs. Stir in the water and mix to form a dough.

2 Roll out the pastry on to a lightly floured surface. Using a 3 inch cookie cutter, stamp out 12 rounds from the pastry and line a patty pan.

3 To make the filling, whisk together the beaten egg, light cream, grated cheese and chopped scallions in a mixing pitcher. Season to taste with salt and cayenne pepper.

4 Pour the filling mixture into the pie shells and bake in a preheated oven, 350°F, for about 20-25 minutes or until the filling is just set. Serve the mini tarts warm or cold.

COOK'S TIP

If you use 6 oz of ready-made shortcrust pastry instead of making it yourself, these tarts can be made in minutes.

VARIATION

Top each mini tartlet with slices of fresh tomato before baking, if you prefer.

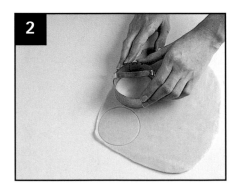

Lentil & Red Bell Pepper Flan

*This savory flan combines lentils and red bell peppers in a tasty whole-wheat pie shell.
This flan is suitable for vegans.*

Serves 6-8

INGREDIENTS

PASTRY:
1³/₄ cups plain whole-wheat flour
¹/₃ cup vegan margarine, cut into
small pieces
4 tbsp water

FILLING:
6 oz red lentils, rinsed
¹/₄ cups vegetable stock
3 tsp vegan margarine
1 onion, chopped

2 red bell peppers, cored, seeded, and
diced
1 tsp yeast extract
1 tbsp tomato paste
3 tbsp chopped fresh parsley
pepper

1 To make the pastry, place the flour in a mixing bowl and rub in the vegan margarine with your fingertips until the mixture resembles fine bread crumbs. Stir in the water and bring together to form a dough. Wrap and chill for 30 minutes.

2 Meanwhile, make the filling. Put the lentils in a saucepan with the stock, bring to a boil and then simmer for 10 minutes until the lentils are tender and can be mashed to a purée.

3 Melt the margarine in a small pan, add the chopped onion and diced red bell peppers and fry until just soft.

4 Add the lentil purée, yeast extract, tomato paste and parsley. Season with pepper. Mix until well combined.

5 On a lightly floured surface, roll out the dough and line a 9½ inch loose-bottomed quiche pan. Prick the base of the pastry with a fork and spoon the lentil

mixture into the pie shell.

6 Bake in a preheated oven, 400°F, for 30 minutes until the filling is firm.

VARIATION

*Add corn to the flan in
step 4 for a colorful and tasty
change, if you prefer.*

Brazil Nut & Mushroom Pie

The button mushrooms give this wholesome vegan pie a wonderful aromatic flavor. The pie can be frozen uncooked and baked from frozen.

Serves 4-6

INGREDIENTS

PASTRY:
1³/₄ cups plain whole-wheat flour
¹/₃ cup vegan margarine, cut into small pieces
4 tbsp water
soya milk, to glaze

FILLING:
6 tsp vegan margarine
1 onion, chopped
1 garlic clove, chopped finely
4¹/₂ oz button mushrooms, sliced
1 tbsp all-purpose flour
²/₃ cup vegetable stock

1 tbsp tomato paste
6 oz brazil nuts, chopped
2³/₄ oz fresh whole-wheat bread crumbs
2 tbsp chopped fresh parsley
¹/₂ tsp pepper

1 To make the pastry, place the flour in a mixing bowl and rub in the vegan margarine with your fingertips until the mixture resembles fine bread crumbs. Stir in the water and bring together to form a dough. Wrap and chill for 30 minutes.

2 To make the filling, melt half of the margarine in a skillet. Add the onion, garlic and mushrooms and fry for 5 minutes until soft. Add the flour and cook for 1 minute, stirring frequently. Gradually add the stock, stirring until the sauce is smooth and beginning to thicken. Stir in the tomato paste, brazil nuts, bread crumbs, parsley, and pepper. Leave to cool slightly.

3 On a lightly floured surface, roll out two thirds of the pastry and use to line a 8 inch loose-bottomed flan pan or pie dish. Spread the filling in the pie shell. Brush the edges of the pastry with soya milk. Roll out the remaining pastry to fit the top of the pie. Seal the edges, make a slit in the top of the pastry and brush with soya milk.

4 Bake in a preheated oven, 400°F, for 30-40 minutes until golden brown.

Garlic & Sage Bread

*This freshly made bread is an ideal accompaniment
to salads and is suitable for vegans.*

Serves 4-6

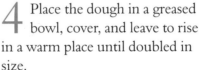

INGREDIENTS

2¼ cups bread brown bread flour
1 envelope quick-rising dried yeast

3 tbsp chopped fresh sage
2 tsp sea salt
3 garlic cloves, chopped finely

1 tsp honey
²/₃ cup tepid water

1 Grease a baking sheet. Sift the flour into a large mixing bowl and stir in the husks remaining in the sifter.

2 Stir in the dried yeast, sage, and half of the sea salt. Reserve 1 teaspoon of the chopped garlic for sprinkling and stir the rest into the bowl. Add the honey with the tepid water and mix together to form a dough.

3 Turn the dough out on to a lightly floured surface and knead it for about 5 minutes (alternatively, use an electric mixer with a dough hook).

4 Place the dough in a greased bowl, cover, and leave to rise in a warm place until doubled in size.

5 Knead the dough again for a few minutes, shape it into a circle (see Cook's Tip) and place on the baking sheet.

6 Cover and leave to rise for a further 30 minutes or until springy to the touch. Sprinkle with the rest of the sea salt and garlic.

7 Bake in a preheated oven, 400°F, for 25-30 minutes. Leave to cool on a wire rack before

COOK'S TIP

*Roll the dough into a long
sausage and then curve it into
a circular shape.*

VARIATION

*Omit the sea salt for sprinkling over
the top of the bread, if preferred.*

Candies & Drinks

There is nothing quite as nice as home-made chocolates and candies – they leave the average box of chocolates in the shade!

You'll find recipes in this chapter to suit everybody's taste. Wonderful, rich, melt-in-the-mouth chocolate truffles, crispy florentines, nutty chocolate creams, and rich chocolate liqueurs – they're all here. There is even some simple-to-make chocolate fudge, so there is no need to fiddle about with sugar thermometers.

Looking for something to wash it all down? We have included two delightfully cool summer chocolate drinks that will simply put bought chocolate drinks to shame. Enjoy!

Chocolate Liqueurs

These tasty chocolate cups are filled with a delicious liqueur-flavored filling. They are a little fiddly to make but lots of fun! Use your favourite liqueur to flavor the cream.

Makes 20

INGREDIENTS

3^1/$_2$ oz dark chocolate
about 5 candied cherries, halved
about 10 hazelnuts or macadamia
    nuts

^{2}/$_3$ cup heavy cream
2 tbsp confectioners' sugar
4 tbsps liqueur

TO FINISH:
1^3/$_4$ oz dark chocolate, melted
a little white chocolate, melted or
    white chocolate curls (see page 50)
    or extra nuts and cherries

1 Line a baking sheet with a sheet of baking parchment. Melt the chocolate and spoon it into 20 paper candy cases, spreading up the sides with a small spoon or pastry brush. Place upside down on the prepared baking sheet and leave to set.

2 Carefully peel away the paper cases. Place a cherry or nut in the base of each cup.

3 To make the filling, place the heavy cream in a mixing bowl and sift the confectioners' sugar on top. Whisk the cream until it is just holding its shape, then whisk in the liqueur.

4 Place the cream in a pastry bag fitted with a ^{1}/$_2$ inch plain tip and pipe a little into each chocolate case. Leave to chill for 20 minutes.

5 To finish, spoon the melted dark chocolate over the cream to cover it and pipe the melted white chocolate on top, swirling it into the dark chocolate with a toothpick. Leave to harden.

Alternatively, cover the cream with the melted dark chocolate and decorate with white chocolate curls before setting. Or, place a small piece of nut or cherry on top of the cream and then cover with dark chocolate.

COOK'S TIP

Candy cases can vary in size. Use the smallest you can find for this recipe.

Chocolate Cherries

These tasty cherry and marzipan candy are simple to make. Serve as petits fours at the end of a meal or for an indulgent nibble at any time of the day.

Serves 4

INGREDIENTS

12 candied cherries
2 tbsp rum or brandy

9 oz marzipan
5 1/2 oz dark chocolate

extra milk, dark or white chocolate,
to decorate (optional)

1 Line a baking sheet smoothly with a sheet of baking parchment.

2 Cut the cherries in half and place in a small bowl. Add the rum or brandy and stir to coat. Leave the cherries to soak for at least 1 hour, stirring occasionally.

3 Divide the marzipan into 24 pieces and roll each piece into a ball. Press half a cherry into the top of each marzipan ball.

4 Break the chocolate into pieces, place in a bowl and set over a pan of hot water. Stir until the chocolate has melted.

5 Dip each candy into the melted chocolate, allowing the excess to drip back into the bowl. Place the coated cherries on the baking parchment and chill until set.

6 If liked, melt a little extra chocolate and drizzle it over the top of the coated cherries. Leave to set.

VARIATION

Flatten the marzipan and use it to mold around the cherries to cover them, then dip in the chocolate as above.

VARIATION

Use a whole almond in place of the halved candied cherries and omit the rum or brandy.

Chocolate Marzipans

These delightful little morsels make the perfect gift,
if you can resist eating them all yourself!

Makes about 30

INGREDIENTS

1 lb marzipan
$^{1}/_{3}$ cup candied cherries, chopped
   very finely
1 oz fresh ginger, chopped very finely

1$^{3}/_{4}$ oz no-soak dried apricots,
   chopped very finely
12 oz dark chocolate
1 oz white chocolate

confectioners' sugar, to dust

1 Line a baking sheet with a sheet of baking parchment. Divide the marzipan into 3 balls and knead each ball to soften it.

2 Work the candied cherries into one portion of the marzipan by kneading on a surface lightly dusted with confectioners' sugar.

3 Do the same with the fresh ginger and another portion of marzipan and then the apricots and the third portion of marzipan.

4 Form each flavored portion of marzipan into small balls, ensuring you keep the different flavors separate.

5 Melt the dark chocolate. Dip one of each flavored ball of marzipan into the chocolate by spiking each one with a toothpick or small skewer, allowing the excess chocolate to drip back into the bowl.

6 Carefully place the balls in clusters of the three flavors on the prepared baking sheet. Repeat

with the remaining marzipan balls. Chill until set.

7 Melt the white chocolate and drizzle a little over the tops of each cluster of marzipan balls. Chill until hardened, then remove from the baking parchment and dust with sugar to serve.

VARIATION

Coat the marzipan balls in white or milk chocolate and drizzle with dark chocolate, if you prefer.

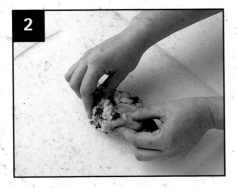

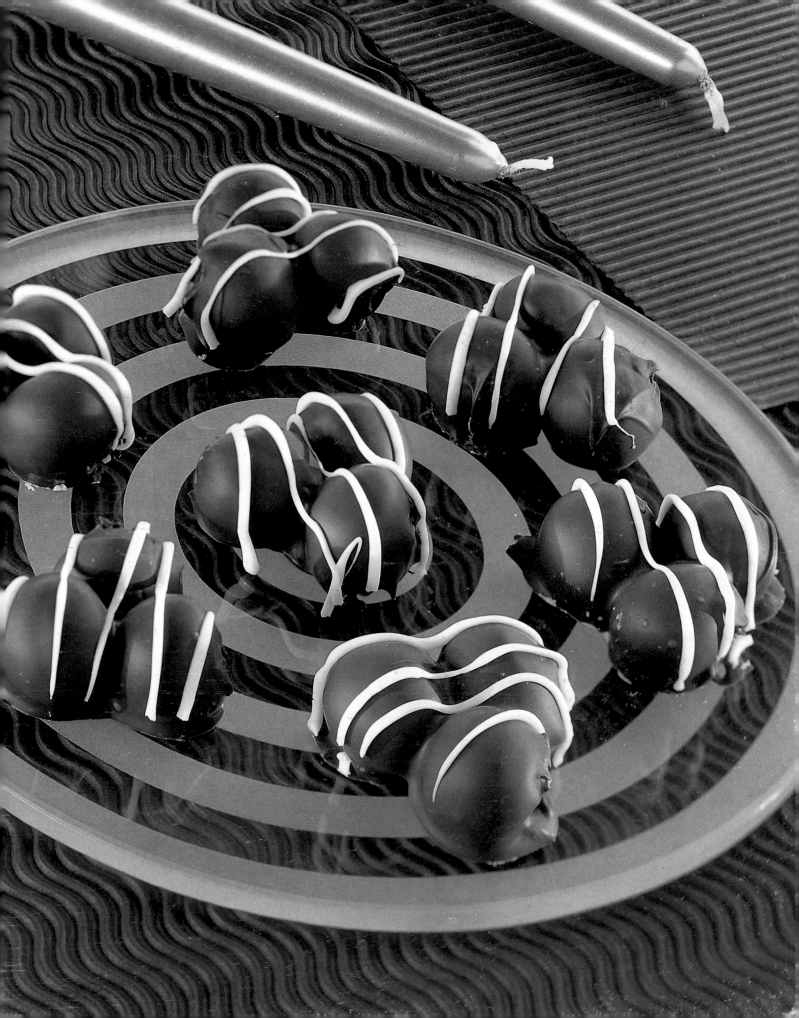

Chocolate Cups with Mascarpone Filling

*Mascarpone – the velvety smooth Italian cheese – makes a
rich, creamy filling for these tasty chocolates*

Makes 20

INGREDIENTS

3¹/₂ oz dark chocolate

FILLING:
3¹/₂ oz milk or dark chocolate
¹/₄ tsp vanilla extract

7 oz mascarpone cheese
cocoa powder, to dust

1 Line a baking sheet with a sheet of baking parchment. Melt the chocolate and spoon it into 20 paper candy cases, spreading up the sides with a small spoon or pastry brush. Place upside down on the prepared baking sheet and leave to set.

2 When set, carefully peel away the paper cases.

3 To make the filling, melt the dark or milk chocolate. Place the mascarpone cheese in a bowl and beat in the vanilla extract and melted chocolate and beat until well combined. Leave the mixture to chill, beating occasionally until firm enough to pipe.

4 Place the mascarpone filling in a pastry bag fitted with a star tip and pipe the mixture into the cups. Decorate with a dusting of cocoa powder.

COOK'S TIP

Mascarpone is a rich Italian soft cheese made from fresh cream, so it has a high fat content. Its delicate flavor blends well with chocolate.

VARIATION

You can use lightly whipped heavy cream instead of the mascarpone cheese, if preferred.

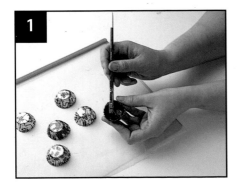

Nutty Chocolate Clusters

*Nuts and crisp cookies encased in chocolate make
these candies rich, chocolatey, and quite irresistible!*

Makes about 30

INGREDIENTS

6 oz white chocolate
3^1/$_2$ oz graham crackers

3^1/$_2$ oz macadamia nuts or brazil
nuts, chopped

1 oz fresh ginger, chopped (optional)
6 oz dark chocolate

1 Line a baking sheet with a sheet of baking parchment. Break the white chocolate into small pieces and place in a large mixing bowl set over a pan of gently simmering water; stir until melted.

2 Break the graham crackers into small pieces. Stir the graham crackers into the melted chocolate with the chopped nuts and fresh ginger, if using.

3 Place heaped teaspoons of the mixture on to the prepared baking sheet.

4 Chill the mixture until set, then carefully remove from the baking parchment.

5 Melt the dark chocolate and leave it to cool slightly. Dip the clusters into the melted chocolate, allowing the excess to drip back into the bowl. Return the clusters to the baking sheet and chill in the refrigerator until set.

COOK'S TIP

The clusters can be stored for up to 1 week in a cool, dry place.

COOK'S TIP

Macadamia and brazil nuts are both rich and high in fat, which makes them particularly popular for confectionery, but other nuts can be used, if preferred.

Easy Chocolate Fudge

This is the easiest fudge to make – for a really rich flavor, use a good dark chocolate with a high cocoa content, ideally at least 70 per cent.

Makes 25-30 pieces

INGREDIENTS

1 lb dark chocolate
1/3 cup unsalted butter

14 oz can sweetened condensed milk

1/2 tsp vanilla extract

1 Lightly grease a 8 inch square cake pan.

2 Break the chocolate into pieces and place in a large saucepan with the butter and condensed milk.

3 Heat gently, stirring until the chocolate and butter melts and the mixture is smooth. Do not allow to boil.

4 Remove from the heat. Beat in the vanilla extract, then beat the mixture for a few minutes until thickened. Pour it into the prepared pan and level the top.

5 Chill the mixture in the refrigerator until firm.

6 Tip the fudge out on to a chopping board and cut into squares to serve.

VARIATION

For chocolate peanut fudge, replace 4 tbsp of the butter with crunchy peanut butter.

COOK'S TIP

Do not use milk chocolate as the results will be too sticky.

COOK'S TIP

Store the fudge in an airtight container in a cool, dry place for up to 1 month. Do not freeze.

No-Cook Fruit & Nut Chocolate Fudge

Chocolate, nuts, and dried fruit – the perfect combination – are all found in this simple-to-make fudge.

Makes about 25 pieces

INGREDIENTS

9 oz dark chocolate

2 tbsp butter

4 tbsp evaporated milk

3 cups confectioners' sugar, sifted

$1/2$ cup roughly chopped hazelnuts

$1/3$ cup golden raisins

1 Lightly grease a 8 inch square cake pan.

2 Break the chocolate into pieces and place it in a bowl with the butter and evaporated milk. Set the bowl over a pan of gently simmering water and stir until the chocolate and butter have melted and the ingredients are well combined.

3 Remove the bowl from the heat and gradually beat in the confectioners' sugar. Stir the hazelnuts and golden raisins into the mixture. Press the fudge into the prepared pan and level the top. Chill until firm.

4 Tip the fudge out on to a chopping board and cut into squares. Place in paper candy cases. Chill until required.

COOK'S TIP

The fudge can be stored in an airtight container for up to 2 weeks.

VARIATION

Vary the nuts used in this recipe; try making the fudge with almonds, brazil nuts, walnuts, or pecans.

Rocky Road Bites

*Young children will love these chewy bites. You can vary the ingredients
and use different nuts and dried fruit according to taste.*

Makes 18

INGREDIENTS

4¹/₂ oz milk chocolate
2¹/₂ oz mini multi-colored
  marshmallows

¹/₄ cup chopped walnuts

1 oz no-soak apricots, chopped

1 Line a baking sheet with baking parchment and set aside.

2 Break the milk chocolate into small pieces and place in a large mixing bowl. Set the bowl over a pan of simmering water and stir until the chocolate has melted.

3 Stir in the marshmallows, walnuts and apricots and toss in the melted chocolate until well covered.

4 Place heaped teaspoons of the mixture on to the prepared baking sheet.

5 Leave the candies to chill in the refrigerator until set.

6 Once they are set, carefully remove the candies from the baking parchment.

7 The chewy bites can be placed in paper candy cases to serve, if desired.

COOK'S TIP

*These candies can be
stored in a cool, dry place for up
to 2 weeks.*

VARIATION

*Light, fluffy marshmallows are
available in white or pastel
colors. If you cannot find mini
marshmallows, use large ones and
snip them into smaller pieces with
kitchen scissors before mixing them
into the melted chocolate
in step 3.*

Collettes

*A creamy, orange-flavored chocolate filling in white
chocolate cups makes a wonderful treat.*

Makes 20

INGREDIENTS

3¹/₂ oz white chocolate

FILLING:
5¹/₂ oz orange-flavored dark
  chocolate
²/₃ cup heavy cream
2 tbsp confectioners' sugar

1 Line a baking sheet with a sheet of baking parchment. Melt the chocolate and spoon it into 20 paper candy cases, spreading up the sides with a small spoon or pastry brush. Place upside down on the prepared baking sheet and leave to set.

2 When set, carefully peel away the paper cases.

3 To make the filling, melt the orange-flavored chocolate and place in a mixing bowl with the heavy cream and the confectioners' sugar. Beat until smooth. Chill until the mixture becomes firm enough to pipe, stirring occasionally.

4 Place the filling in a pastry bag fitted with a star tip and pipe a little into each case. Leave to chill until required.

COOK'S TIP

*Use the smallest candy cases you
can find for these cups.*

COOK'S TIP

*If they do not hold their shape well,
use 2 cases to make a double
thickness mold. Foil cases are firmer
so use these if you
can find them.*

VARIATION

*Add 1 tbsp orange-flavored liqueur
to the filling, if preferred.*

Mini Chocolate Cones

These unusual cone-shaped chocolates make an interesting change from the more usual cup shape. Filled with a mint-flavored cream, they are perfect for an after-dinner chocolate.

Makes 10

INGREDIENTS

2³/₄ oz dark chocolate
¹/₃ cup heavy cream
1 tbsp confectioners' sugar

1 tbsp crème de menthe
chocolate coffee beans, to decorate
(optional)

1 Cut ten 3 inch circles of baking parchment. Shape each circle into a cone shape and secure with sticky tape.

2 Melt the chocolate. Using a small pastry brush or clean artists' brush, brush the inside of each cone with melted chocolate.

3 Brush a second layer of chocolate on the inside of the cones and leave to chill until set. Carefully peel away the paper.

4 Place the heavy cream, confectioners' sugar, and crème de menthe in a mixing bowl and whip until just holding its shape. Place in a pastry bag fitted with a star tip and pipe the mixture into the chocolate cones.

5 Decorate the cones with chocolate coffee beans (if using) and chill until required.

COOK'S TIP

The chocolate cones can be made in advance and kept in the refrigerator for up to 1 week. Do not fill them more than 2 hours before you are going to serve them.

VARIATION

Use a different flavored liqueur to flavor the cream: a coffee-flavored liqueur is perfect. If you want a mint flavor without using a liqueur, use a few drops of peppermint extract to flavor the cream according to taste.

Mini Chocolate Tartlets

Small pie shells are filled with a rich chocolate filling to serve as petits fours. Use mini muffin pans or small individual tartlet pans to make the pie shells.

Serves 4

INGREDIENTS

$1^1/_2$ cups all-purpose flour
$1/_3$ cup butter
1 tbsp superfine sugar
about 1 tbsp water

FILLING:
$3^1/_2$ oz full-fat soft cheese
5 tsp superfine sugar
1 small egg, lightly beaten
$1^3/_4$ oz dark chocolate

TO DECORATE:
$1/_3$ cup heavy cream
dark chocolate curls (see page 50)
cocoa powder, to dust

1 Sift the flour into a mixing bowl. Cut the butter into small pieces and rub in with your fingertips until the mixture resembles fine bread crumbs. Stir in the sugar. Add enough water to mix to a soft dough, then cover and chill for 15 minutes.

2 Roll out the pastry on a lightly floured surface and use to line 18 mini tartlet pans or mini muffin pans. Prick the bases with a toothpick.

3 Beat together the full-fat soft cheese and the sugar. Beat in the egg. Melt the chocolate and beat it into the mixture. Spoon into the pie shells and bake in a preheated oven, 375°F, for 15 minutes until the pastry is crisp and the filling set. Place the pans on a wire rack to cool completely.

4 Chill the tartlets. Whip the cream until it is just holding its shape. Place in a pastry bag fitted with a star tip. Pipe rosettes of cream on top of the tartlets.

Decorate with chocolate curls and dust with cocoa powder.

COOK'S TIP

The tartlets can be made up to 3 days ahead. Decorate on the day of serving, preferably no more than 4 hours in advance.

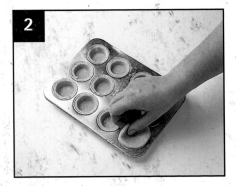

Mini Florentines

These classic cookies can be served with desserts but they also make delightful petits fours. *Serve at the end of a meal with coffee, or arrange in a shallow presentation box for an attractive gift.*

Makes about 40

INGREDIENTS

¹/₃ cup butter

¹/₃ cup superfine sugar

2 tbsp golden raisins or raisins

2 tbsp candied cherries, chopped

2 tbsp crystalized ginger, chopped

1 oz sunflower seeds

³/₄ cup slivered almonds

2 tbsp heavy cream

6 oz dark or milk chocolate

1 Lightly grease and flour 2 baking sheets or line with baking parchment. Place the butter in a small pan and heat gently until melted. Add the sugar, stir until dissolved, then bring the mixture to a boil. Remove from the heat and stir in the golden raisins or raisins, cherries, ginger, sunflower seeds, and almonds. Mix well, then beat in the cream.

2 Place small teaspoons of the fruit and nut mixture on to the prepared baking sheet, allowing plenty of space for the mixture to spread. Bake in a preheated oven, 350°F, for 10-12 minutes until light golden in color.

3 Remove from the oven and, whilst still hot, use a circular cookie cutter to pull in the edges to form a perfect circle. Leave to cool and crispen before removing from the baking sheet.

4 Melt most of the chocolate and spread it on a sheet of baking parchment. When the chocolate is on the point of setting, place the cookies flat-side down on the chocolate and leave to harden completely.

5 Cut around the florentines and remove from the paper. Spread a little more chocolate on the already coated side of the florentines and use a fork to mark waves in the chocolate. Leave to set. Arrange the florentines on a plate (or in a presentation box for a gift) with alternate sides facing upwards. Keep cool.

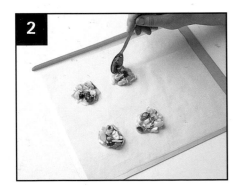

Italian Chocolate Truffles

These tasty little morsels are flavored with almonds and chocolate, and are simplicity itself to make. Served with coffee, they are the perfect end to a meal.

Makes about 24

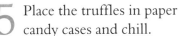

INGREDIENTS

6 oz dark chocolate
2 tbsp almond-flavored liqueur or
    orange-flavored liqueur
3 tbsp unsalted butter

1³/4 oz confectioners' sugar

1/2 cup ground almonds
1³/4 oz grated chocolate

1 Melt the dark chocolate with the liqueur in a bowl set over a saucepan of hot water, stirring until well combined.

2 Add the butter and stir until it has melted. Stir in the confectioners' sugar and the ground almonds.

3 Leave the mixture in a cool place until firm enough to roll into about 24 balls.

4 Place the grated chocolate on a plate and roll the truffles in the chocolate to coat them.

5 Place the truffles in paper candy cases and chill.

COOK'S TIP

These truffles will keep for about 2 weeks in a cool place.

VARIATION

The almond-flavored liqueur gives these truffles an authentic Italian flavor. The original almond liqueur, Amaretto di Saronno, comes from Saronno in Italy.

VARIATION

For a sweeter truffle, use milk chocolate instead of dark. Dip the truffles in melted chocolate to finish, if desired.

White Chocolate Truffles

These delicious creamy white truffles will testify to the fact that there is nothing quite as nice as home-made chocolates. It is worth buying the best chocolate you can for these truffles.

Makes about 20

INGREDIENTS

2 tbsp unsalted butter
5 tbsp heavy cream
8 oz good quality Swiss white
 chocolate

1 tbsp orange-flavored liqueur
(optional)

TO FINISH:
$3^1/_2$ oz white chocolate

1 Line a jelly roll pan with baking parchment.

2 Place the butter and cream in a small saucepan and bring slowly to a boil, stirring constantly. Boil for 1 minute, then remove from the heat.

3 Break the chocolate into pieces and add to the cream. Stir until melted, then beat in the liqueur, if using.

4 Pour into the prepared pan and chill for about 2 hours until firm.

5 Break off pieces of mixture and roll them into balls. Chill for a further 30 minutes before finishing the truffles.

6 To finish, melt the white chocolate. Dip the balls in the chocolate, allowing the excess to drip back into the bowl. Place on non-stick baking parchment and swirl the chocolate with the prongs of a fork. Leave to harden.

7 Drizzle a little melted dark chocolate over the truffles if you wish and leave to set. Place the truffles in paper cases to serve.

COOK'S TIP

The truffle mixture needs to be firm but not too hard to roll. If the mixture is too hard, allow it to stand at room temperature for a few minutes to soften slightly. During rolling the mixture will become sticky but will reharden in the refrigerator before coating.

COOK'S TIP

The chocolates can be kept in the refrigerator for up to 2 weeks.

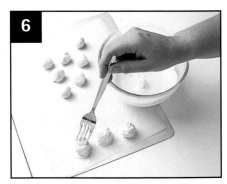

Rum Truffles

*Truffles are always popular. They make a fabulous gift or,
served with coffee, they are a perfect end to a meal.*

Makes about 20

INGREDIENTS

5^1/$_2$ oz dark chocolate
small knob of butter
2 tbsp rum

1^3/$_4$ oz shredded coconut
3^1/$_2$ oz cake crumbs
6 tbsp confectioners' sugar

2 tbsp cocoa powder

1 Break the chocolate into
pieces and place in a bowl
with the butter. Set the bowl over
a pan of gently simmering water,
stir until melted and combined.

2 Remove from the heat and
beat in the rum. Stir in the
shredded coconut, cake crumbs
and 1^3/$_4$ oz of the confectioners'
sugar. Beat until combined. Add a
little extra rum if the mixture is
stiff.

3 Roll the mixture into small
balls and place them on a
sheet of baking parchment. Leave
to chill until firm.

4 Sift the remaining
confectioners' sugar on to a
large plate. Sift the cocoa powder
on to another plate. Roll half of the
truffles in the confectioners' sugar
until coated and roll the remaining
truffles in the cocoa powder.

5 Place the truffles in paper
candy cases and leave to chill
until required.

COOK'S TIP

*These truffles will keep for about
2 weeks in a cool place.*

VARIATION

*Make the truffles with white
chocolate and replace the rum with
coconut liqueur or milk, if you
prefer. Roll them in cocoa powder or
dip in melted milk chocolate.*

Cold Chocolate Drinks

These delicious chocolate summer drinks are perfect for
making a chocoholic's summer day!

Serves 2

INGREDIENTS

CHOCOLATE MILK SHAKE:
2 cups ice cold milk
3 tbsp drinking chocolate powder
3 scoops chocolate ice cream
cocoa powder, to dust (optional)

CHOCOLATE ICE CREAM SODA:
5 tbsp chocolate dessert sauce
soda water
2 scoops of chocolate ice cream
heavy cream, whipped

dark or milk chocolate, grated

1 To make Chocolate Milk Shake, place half of the ice-cold milk in a blender.

2 Add the drinking chocolate powder to the blender and 1 scoop of the chocolate ice cream. Blend until the mixture is frothy and well mixed. Stir in the remaining milk.

3 Place the remaining 2 scoops of chocolate ice cream in 2 serving glasses and carefully pour the chocolate milk over the ice cream.

4 Sprinkle a little cocoa powder (if using) over the top of each drink and serve at once.

5 To make Chocolate Ice Cream Soda, divide the chocolate dessert sauce between 2 glasses. (You can use a ready-made chocolate dessert sauce, or the Hot Chocolate Sauce on page 160, or the Glossy Chocolate Sauce on page 188.)

6 Add a little soda water to each glass and stir to combine the sauce and soda water. Place a scoop of ice cream in each glass and top up with more soda water.

7 Place a dollop of whipped double cream on the top, if liked, then sprinkle the cream with a little grated dark or milk chocolate.

COOK'S TIP

Served in a tall glass, a milk shake
or an ice cream soda makes a
scrumptious snack in a drink.
Serve with straws, if wished.

Hot Chocolate Drinks

*Rich and soothing, a hot chocolate drink in the evening can be just
what you need to help ease away the stresses of the day.*

Serves 4

INGREDIENTS

SPICY HOT CHOCOLATE:
2$^1/_2$ cups milk
1 tsp ground mixed allspice
3$^1/_2$ oz dark chocolate
4 cinnamon sticks
$^1/_3$ cup heavy cream, lightly whipped

HOT CHOCOLATE & ORANGE TODDY:
2$^1/_2$ oz orange-flavored dark
  chocolate
2$^1/_2$ cups milk
3 tbsp rum
2 tbsp heavy cream

grated nutmeg

1 To make the Spicy Hot Chocolate, pour the milk into a small pan. Sprinkle in the allspice.

2 Break the dark chocolate into squares and add to the milk. Heat the mixture over a low heat until the milk is just boiling, stirring all the time to prevent the milk burning on the bottom of the pan.

3 Place 2 cinnamon sticks in 2 cups and pour in the spicy hot chocolate. Top with the whipped heavy cream and serve.

4 To make Hot Chocolate & Orange Toddy, break the orange-flavored dark chocolate into squares and place in a small saucepan with the milk. Heat over a low heat until just boiling, stirring constantly.

5 Remove the pan from the heat and stir in the rum. Pour into cups.

6 Pour the cream over the back of a spoon or swirl on to the top so that it sits on top of the hot chocolate. Sprinkle with grated nutmeg and serve at once.

COOK'S TIP

Using a cinnamon stick as a stirrer will give any hot chocolate drink a sweet, pungent flavor of cinnamon without overpowering the flavor of the chocolate.

Index